*The Absolute Best*

# MUG CAKES

## COOKBOOK

*The Absolute Best Mug Cakes Cookbook*
## Quick Start Guide

HUNGRY?
TURN TO PAGE 147 FOR CHOCOLATE CHIP

FAMILY NIGHT?
TURN TO PAGE 75 FOR CARAMEL APPLE

WANT TO IMPRESS YOUR FRIENDS?
TURN TO PAGE 129 FOR CHOCOLATE-MERLOT

ON A DIET?
TURN TO PAGE 137 FOR LOW-CARB COCONUT

# THE
# ABSOLUTE BEST
# MUG
# CAKES
# COOKBOOK

### 100+ *Family-Friendly Microwave Cakes*

**ROCKRIDGE
PRESS**

Photography © 2015 by Rachel Ballard

ISBN: Print 978-1-62315-580-3 | eBook 978-1-62315-581-0

# Contents

......................

INTRODUCTION 7

CHAPTER 1
......................
*The Basics 9*

CHAPTER 2
......................
*Take It up a Notch 19*

CHAPTER 3
......................
*The Classics 31*

CHAPTER 4
......................
*Chocolate, Chocolate
Everywhere 45*

CHAPTER 5
......................
*Get Fruity 57*

CHAPTER 6
......................
*Seasonal Favorites 69*

CHAPTER 7
......................
*Birthdays 81*

CHAPTER 8
......................
*Holidays 95*

CHAPTER 9
......................
*Cake for Breakfast 109*

CHAPTER 10
......................
*For the Grown-Ups 121*

CHAPTER 11
......................
*Mug Cakes for
Special Diets 133*

CHAPTER 12
......................
*Beyond Cakes 143*

CHAPTER 13
......................
*Frostings, Toppings,
and Glazes 155*

COMMON FOOD SUBSTITUTIONS 173

MEASUREMENT CONVERSIONS 178

SOURCES FOR INGREDIENTS 179

REFERENCES 180

INDEX 181

# *Introduction*

...........................................

WHO DOESN'T ENJOY CAKE? It's like eating a bite of love.

But nothing makes your shoulders slump more than having a cake craving only to realize just how much time it will take to measure all the ingredients, find the mixer, cream the butter, scrape down the bowl, sneeze your way through a cloud of flour, and then wait for what seems like forever as the cake bakes and then cools.

Enter one of the most fun additions to your kitchen repertoire: mug cakes. These single-serving treats can be made in a matter of minutes, in a regular ol' coffee mug. Best of all, there's almost no mess to clean up afterward.

Think of a warm, gooey chocolate cake to go with your afternoon coffee when it's time for a work break. Or an after-school snack for the kids while they do their homework. Mug cakes are so easy that even younger children can make them with adult supervision. You can even have a mug cake cook-off on family nights and see who wins a taste test!

This book takes you by the hand and shows you how to make a variety of delicious mug cakes. It doesn't matter if you're known as the anti-baker—you'll have no trouble making any of the recipes on these pages. You'll find out how to choose the perfect container for baking your cake (hint: sometimes jelly jars work better) and how to adjust the recipe to get the exact texture you're looking for in your cake. Tips and tricks are given throughout the book, and there are even suggestions for throwing delightful mug cake parties. With mug cakes, everyone in the family can make their very own dessert tailored to suit individual tastes and dietary restrictions, so no one has to be left out of the fun.

Be warned: Mug cakes are addictive. They are so much fun to make that you might find you can't stop. You probably have everything you need to make your first cake in a mug right in your kitchen. So what are you waiting for?

# 1

# *The Basics*

MUG CAKES ARE DEFINITELY ONE OF THE EASIEST desserts you'll ever make. There aren't many ingredients, and the measuring is minimal, so you can get right to work with the important stuff—eating a delicious homemade cake! There are lots of reasons to love mug cakes. Here are a few:

* They are easy to make for cooks of all ages. Young children will need some adult supervision when they're using the microwave, but they can do the mixing and measuring themselves. Added bonus? It's a wonderful way to teach measurements and fractions to children!

* A mug cake is a great way to create a yummy dessert fast. There's no need to wait for the oven to preheat or the cake to be baked, cooled, and frosted. Set your microwave for a minute or two and it's ready to go.

* No more arguing over whether to make chocolate or vanilla or who gets to lick the spoon. Mug cakes allow everyone to pick exactly the flavor they want, top it with their favorite toppings, and lick their own spoons. Dessert is a great way to encourage the family to linger at the table and talk after dinner, too.

* Single-serving batches make portion control easy and let the whole family eat healthier. These snacks are self-limiting. Once you eat your mug cake, you're done. Leftover cake won't be sitting around, beckoning you with its sugary siren song.

* Cleanup is also super easy. You only use a mug, a spoon, a bowl, and maybe a measuring spoon or two. You'll just need to give the countertop a quick wipe down and put the utensils in the dishwasher.

* There are so many different kinds of mug cakes that you won't ever get bored with them! The most difficult decision is which flavor you want to make first. Will it be mocha with a ganache glaze or carrot cake with cream cheese frosting?

* You can make them anywhere you have access to a microwave. Whether you are at work, in the dorm, or at home, your favorite cake is just minutes away.

* Put a pretty mug, a container of homemade mug cake mix, and some instructions in a basket tied with ribbon for a creative homemade gift anyone would appreciate.

* Once you learn the basics of how to make mug cakes, you can create your own recipes. Combine ingredients to make your favorite flavor combinations, whether that's cinnamon-mocha or something no one has thought of before.

* Mug cakes aren't just for dessert. You can whip up a quick coffee cake, muffin, or doughnut in a mug for a quick, delicious breakfast on the go.

* It's fun!

## The Ingredients

Since mug cakes are designed to be quick, easy, and fun, the ingredients list is usually quite short. Once you know what the basic ingredients are, you'll be able to adjust them and experiment with different additions to get exactly the flavor you want. It's always best to bring your ingredients to room temperature before beginning your cake. The cake will be easier to mix and will have a far better texture.

### FLOUR

Flour, of any kind, is an essential ingredient you must have to make a mug cake. Generally, self-rising flour is the best choice so you don't have to play around with tiny fractions of baking powder and baking

soda. You can make homemade self-rising flour by sifting together
1 cup cake flour, 1 teaspoon baking powder, and ¼ teaspoon kosher
salt. Then just measure like commercial self-rising flour. If you are
on a special diet, you can substitute gluten-free flour, almond flour, or
a variety of other flours for the self-rising flour in the recipe—just be
sure to add a pinch of gluten-free baking powder.

Cake flour will give you a softer texture than all-purpose flour.
If neither seems quite right, try half cake flour and half all-purpose
flour. Homemade self-rising cake flour will give the cake the softest,
most tender texture.

## BUTTER

Butter should always be unsalted unless the recipe states otherwise.
This gives you control over how much salt is in your cake.

Recipes will almost always call for butter or some other fat. Fat
helps with the cake's texture and moistness. It's much easier to mix in
if it is softened or melted. Try a recipe with softened butter and then
another time with melted butter to see which you prefer.

## EGGS

The eggs used when testing these recipes were large, organic eggs.
Any large hen's egg can be substituted. Egg helps the cake rise prop-
erly and makes it light and airy.

While most recipes in this book use a whole egg, some call for just
the egg yolk or the egg white. The trick to separating the yolk from the
white is having the egg at room temperature.

## MILK

Milk and buttermilk are most often the liquid ingredients called for,
but some recipes may require coffee or another liquid. When milk is
called for it is whole milk unless the recipe states otherwise.

If you're making a dairy-free mug cake, almond milk, soy
milk, coconut milk, or rice milk can be used in place of whole cow's
milk. You can use low-fat or skim milk if you choose, but it may
cause changes in the cake's texture. Adding a teaspoon or so of
butter or another fat can help with that if you prefer a more traditional
cake texture.

# YOUR FIRST MUG CAKE

Consider your first few mug cake experiments. How else will you find out what ingredient types work best for you and give you the results you're looking for? It's a good idea to make notes about the recipes you try, the type of flour you use, and the length of time you bake the cake. Record your thoughts, observations, and results. That way you'll be able to see a pattern over time, and identify the best results. Maybe cooking your cake on 70 percent works better for you than cooking it at a higher power. Your notes can help you figure out what you like and what you don't.

Don't be afraid to experiment with different containers, ingredients, and microwave settings to achieve the exact texture and flavor you want.

## THE MUG

Finding the perfect mug isn't too difficult. Each recipe in this book can be made in two 8- to 12-ounce microwave-safe mugs. Whether your mugs are larger or smaller, fill them only halfway as a rule of thumb. More than halfway when making the cake is asking for trouble. You'll end up with batter spilling over the sides and pooling in the micro-wave, and the promise of an easy cleanup will be out the door. A large, plain ceramic mug is perfect for most of these recipes.

You can certainly use other containers to make your mug cake as well. Basically anything microwave safe is fine—just don't fill the vessel more than halfway. Glass jelly and canning jars work very well and have screw-on tops, making the cakes easy to transport. A paper cup can be used, but you'll need to reduce the microwave time. Thick ceramic can take two minutes or a little more to bake, but a cake in a paper cup will be done in less than a minute. Just remember that whatever container you use, it needs to be food safe as well as micro-wave safe. The recipes in this book were tested with a heavy, ceramic 12-ounce mug.

## THE MICROWAVE

Once you have the mug you want, it's time to turn your attention to the microwave. Microwave ovens come in a variety of wattages. When baking in a microwave, it's important to know which wattage you're working with. These recipes were tested in a 1,000-watt microwave. Your microwave may have less wattage. If that's the case, you may find that you'll have to bake the mug cake a bit longer.

Most microwave ovens allow you to adjust the power setting. Generally the recipes in this book will work fine when microwaved on high. Baking on high for 1½ to 2½ minutes should be just about right. You can also try microwaving at 70 or 80 or 90 percent power to see if it changes the texture of your cake. If you have a microwave that doesn't rotate the food while it's cooking, then you'll also need to turn the mug a couple of times to make sure the cake cooks evenly.

Because of the way they cook, microwaves don't brown food. You can add to the visual appeal and flavor of your mug cakes with one of the frosting, topping, or glaze recipes in Chapter 13.

Finally, always microwave one mug cake at a time. Cooking two at once lengthens the time it takes to cook them and may result in uneven cooking.

## TRIAL RUN

Your first mug cake will take some finessing. Start by cooking the mug cake for 1½ minutes, and if it isn't ready, put it back in the microwave for 10- to 15-second intervals until the cake is as done as you want it. To test the cake to see if it's done, gently touch the top. If it feels firm but springy, then it's done.

You can also use the tried-and-true toothpick method. If a toothpick inserted into the center of the cake comes out clean, it is done— or at least not undercooked. So use caution, and err on the side of undercooked, because an overcooked cake will also pass the toothpick test.

The nature of microwave cooking makes it easy to overcook baked goods. Remember that the cake will cook for a few more minutes as it cools down. If your cake is right on the border between being raw and being done, let it sit on the counter for five minutes and see if it achieves the proper degree of doneness.

## SUGAR

Sugar can be either brown or white. Brown sugar and white granulated sugar can be used interchangeably, with differing results and flavors. Brown sugar will give a little caramel flavor to the cake and keep it a little moister, while white sugar lets the flavor of the cake shine through. It's really up to you. Because these mug cake serving sizes are small, you can also use measure-for-measure sugar substitutes if you wish.

Date sugar can be used in the same measure as sugar. You may even find that you need less. Honey or maple syrup can also be used to sweeten your cakes, but you'll want to cut back on the other liquid in the recipe by about a tablespoon. You may even find you don't need the other liquid.

## SALT

Salt helps bring out the full flavor of food. Kosher salt is the best to use because there are not many impurities in it to change the flavor of your dish. If you don't have kosher salt, then your regular table salt may be substituted.

Sea salt is another possibility. It has even fewer impurities than kosher salt. Sea salt crystals, like pretty pink Himalayan sea salt, can be sprinkled on top of caramel or chocolate cakes to create sensational flavors, as can smoked salt or fleur de sel. Try a few different salts out.

## Tips and Tricks

Yes, mug cakes are ridiculously simple to make, but there are still a few tips and tricks that will make them even more foolproof. You'll discover your own tricks as you gain experience, but here are some guidelines to ensure your success as you evolve from a novice to an expert mug cake maker.

* Always read the recipe instructions carefully before making your mug cake. Make sure you have all the ingredients on hand before you start. Take the time to bring the ingredients to room temperature for the best results.

* Although you can bake the cake in any size mug, wider mugs allow the cake to bake more evenly than tapering or narrow mugs.

* You'll know your mug cake is done when the top is firm but springy when you lightly touch it.

* Uneaten mug cakes can be frozen. Let the cake cool, put it in an airtight container, and freeze for up to three months. You can also run a knife around the inside of the mug when the cake is cool and remove the cake before freezing. (If you plan to do this, grease the inside of the mug with some butter before adding the batter to it.)

* If you are going to make a mug cake with whole-wheat flour, use whole-wheat pastry flour rather than all-purpose whole-wheat flour. Your cake will be lighter and more delicate.

* Because of the way microwaves cook, the top of the cake will never be golden brown the way oven-baked cakes are. If this bothers you, there's an easy fix. Add 1 tablespoon water and 2 tablespoons brown sugar to a microwave-safe bowl. Heat it for 30 seconds and check its texture. If still grainy, continue heating at 10-second intervals until it is no longer grainy. Brush the hot syrup on the top of the cake. It will give a little color to the cake and a little extra sweetness, too.

* Premake your cake mix to make future mug cake baking even faster and easier. Double or triple a recipe, and then mix the dry ingredients together. Put this cake mix in a jar with a tight lid. When you want to make a mug cake, you'll just need to shake the jar to remix the ingredients, measure out the amount called for in the recipe, and add the other ingredients to the mix. You just cut your prep time in half.

* Unsalted butter is the first choice for fat in most recipes, but if you prefer not to use it, then organic, unrefined extra-virgin coconut oil works well, too. It will add a little coconut flavor to the cake, which is pleasant for most people. Other mild oils like peanut or vegetable oil can be substituted.

* Put a microwave-safe plate beneath the mug when you are cooking the cake. It will catch any spills and make cleanup much easier.

* When it comes to toppings, anything goes. It's wonderful to make the easy, homemade toppings (see Chapter 13), but there's nothing wrong with keeping a variety of canned frostings, fruit pie filling, and dessert sauces in the pantry for indulging those cravings that hit you unexpectedly.

Mug cakes are relatively inexpensive, so you can experiment with them without feeling like you've wasted a lot of money if you don't like the results. You can create your own signature mug cake desserts for that same reason. Practice makes perfect!

# TROUBLESHOOTING

**OH NO, IT OVERFLOWED.** The mug was likely more than half-full. Microwaves cause the batter to rise fast and high while it's cooking. Next time add less batter to the mug.

**WHAT GOES UP SHOULDN'T COME DOWN: THE CAKE ROSE AND THEN SANK.** It could be that the cake wasn't all the way done. Next time try microwaving it for 10 more seconds. The top should be firm but springy when touched.

The other possibility is that there's nothing wrong at all. Mug cakes are yummy and fast, but they can't be compared to cakes baked in an oven. Even though the gorgeous images you see everywhere show the mug cake high, light, and beautiful, the truth is that the cakes have a tendency to sink a little when you take them out of the microwave. It doesn't affect the flavor at all—it will still be delicious.

Don't fill the mug with more batter thinking it will help. The only thing that will happen is that the cake will overflow in the microwave and you'll have a mess to clean up. Always keep the cake batter at the halfway level in the mug.

**IT WAS DRY, DRY, DRY.** A dry as dust, overcooked cake is not the way to end your cake craving. The first time you microwave a mug cake, you should cook it for the shortest time listed—usually 1 minute. If it is not cooked at that point, continue to cook it in 1-second intervals until the cake is firm but springy to the touch.

**IT WAS CRUMBLY.** Cakes made without egg will be a bit crumblier than those with it. If the texture of your cake is too crumbly for your tastes, try adding an egg if the recipe doesn't call for one, or omitting the egg if the recipe does call for it. Cakes made with coconut flour will almost always be crumbly to some extent because coconut absorbs more moisture.

**IS IT A CAKE OR A BALL? IT WAS RUBBERY.** A weird, rubbery texture is often caused by overmixing the batter once the flour goes in. All batters should be mixed just until smooth. Flour has a protein in it (gluten) that develops the longer you mix it. When it's gently mixed for a very short period of time, the protein doesn't develop. Also, try using cake flour instead of all-purpose flour, as it has a lower protein content.

# 2

...............

# *Take It up a Notch*

NOW THAT YOU KNOW THE BASICS, let's jump into some of the variations to show you just how versatile these little desserts really are.

## Bake It Old School

If you love the idea of mug cakes but don't have a microwave or prefer not to use one, you don't have to miss out on all the fun. Mug cake recipes can easily be adjusted for baking in an oven or toaster oven. They'll just take longer to bake, but still less time than a full-size cake. You'll need to make sure your mugs are ovenproof. If you have any doubt at all, then use ramekins or large custard cups.

Grease the inside of the mugs carefully with unsalted butter and place them on a cookie sheet. Preheat your oven or toaster oven to 350°F while you measure and mix the cake batter in a small bowl. Spoon the batter into the greased mugs, filling them no more than half full, and then place the cookie sheet with the mugs on it in the oven for 7 to 10 minutes. The cakes are done when a toothpick inserted into the center comes out clean.

You may need to bake your cakes for less time if using a small ramekin or more time if using a larger mug or jelly jar. Always keep an eye on the cakes so they don't overbake.

Making a mug cake in the oven will increase the amount of time you have to wait for that first, sweet bite, but it does have its benefits. An oven-baked cake will be moister and lighter in texture than a cake cooked in the microwave. And more than one oven-baked mug cake can be baked at the same time. So if you're having a mug cake party, oven baking may be the faster way to get those cakes baked.

## Easy Dietary Substitution Tricks

It's difficult to be that one person or have a child who can't eat what everyone else is eating. Mug cakes mean no one has to feel deprived.

Ingredient substitutions can be made easily that will allow everyone to enjoy their cake right along with everyone else. Every mug cake recipe in this book can be adjusted to accommodate special diets, whether gluten-free, sugar-free, or vegan. Remember, you are using such small amounts of ingredients that it isn't costly to experiment until you get exactly what you want.

Here are some common substitutions you can make. All ingredients are substituted measure for measure unless the instructions state otherwise. So the same amount of gluten-free flour can be used in place of regular flour. If there are several possible substitutions—for example, substituting sucralose, xylitol, erythritol, or stevia for sugar—you can choose the one you prefer.

### GLUTEN-FREE

Numerous commercial gluten-free flours are available in most grocery stores and supermarkets. You can also make your own gluten-free flour by combining 6 cups brown rice flour, 2 cups potato starch, and 1 cup tapioca flour. Mix well and store in an airtight container in your pantry. Use it in equal measure for any of the wheat-based flours called for in a recipe.

### SUGAR-FREE

Sugar substitutes need to be heat-stable; otherwise, you'll find that your cake won't taste very good. Sugar substitutes will add the expected sweetness to your mug cake, but you may end up with a slightly different cake texture. Most, but not all, sweeteners can be used measure for measure in place of sugar because the mug cakes are so small. Here are some possibilities:

* Xylitol is a natural sugar alcohol. It does not affect the body like regular sugar. It can have uncomfortable digestive side effects,

so use it sparingly until you know what your tolerance is. It can be used measure for measure in place of sugar.

* Erythritol is another natural sugar alcohol similar to xylitol but less likely to cause digestive problems. It can be used measure for measure in place of sugar.

* Stevia is the derivative of the stevia leaf. Like other sugar substitutes, it has no effect on blood sugar. It is highly concentrated, so it cannot be used in the same measure as sugar. You'll need to experiment to see how much you need in your cake. It works well in combination with other sweeteners.

* Sucralose is manufactured in a form that can be used measure for measure as sugar. It is an artificial sweetener, and some people believe it poses health risks.

Aspartame and other sweeteners that aren't mentioned here are not heat stable and therefore will not work well for baking. Note that some of the recipes in this book call for diet soda as a possible substitution; if you choose to use these, make sure they do not contain aspartame or any other sweetener not on the preceding list.

## DAIRY-FREE

There are a variety of milk substitutes, and all of them work well in mug cakes. Some of the more common substitutions include:

* Almond milk

* Coconut milk

* Soy milk

* Rice milk

Organic, extra-virgin coconut oil is a fantastic substitute for the butter in these recipes. Make sure it is organic because other coconut oils are highly processed and very unhealthy. The best choice for health and nutrition is organic unrefined coconut oil, but it has a more pronounced coconut flavor. Organic refined oil is fine and may be cheaper. Other nondairy substitutes include soy butter and various vegan butters that you can find in natural foods stores. You could use margarine, but it doesn't give the quality and flavor to baked goods that other fats do.

# MAKE YOUR OWN GLUTEN-FREE FLOUR MIXTURE

You'll want to experiment with gluten-free flour on several recipes before you decide on one. The ingredients are often very different, which means that the finished product will be different for each one, too. Gluten-free flour substitutes using brown rice tend to be sweeter than those using corn flour, for example. Coconut flour tends to soak up the moisture in baked goods and may result in an odd texture if you aren't careful.

All low-carb flour substitutes are gluten-free, but not all gluten-free flours are low-carb. It's important that you read a recipe through before you make it and double-check anything you don't think fits into your eating plan. If you have doubts, leave it out.

No one flour substitute is necessarily better than another—experiment to see which you like best. Because mug cakes are small, all flour alternatives should measure cup for cup with regular flour. It's always best to experiment to find the right amount to suit your tastes.

If you make your own gluten-free flour combination, always mix the flour well before using. If the ingredients aren't evenly distributed, the finished cake result will not be successful. Each of these gluten-free flours can be kept in airtight containers in the pantry for months at a time.

## GLUTEN-FREE, SELF-RISING FLOUR MIX #1

Makes 7 cups / Prep time: 5 minutes

This is a good all-purpose mix that works well with most of the mug cake recipes.

In a large bowl, combine 4½ cups each brown rice flour, white rice flour, sweet rice flour, and tapioca flour, and mix in 2½ tablespoons xanthan gum (it helps with texture). Add 2 tablespoons gluten-free baking powder and 1 teaspoon kosher salt and stir to incorporate well.

Store in an airtight container. Mix well before each use.

## GLUTEN-FREE, SELF-RISING FLOUR MIX #2

Makes 18¼ cups / Prep time: 5 minutes

This is a light, bland mix that works well for vanilla and other delicately flavored cakes.

In a large bowl, mix together 9 cups white rice flour, 4 cups sweet rice flour, 2 cups cornstarch, and 3 cups potato flour. Mix in 2 tablespoons xanthan gum, 2 tablespoons gluten-free baking powder, and 1 teaspoon kosher salt.

Store in an airtight container. Mix well before each use.

## GLUTEN-FREE, SELF-RISING FLOUR MIX #3

Makes 9¼ cups / Prep time: 5 minutes

This mix contains nut flour, which adds a little fat, so you may want to cut any other fat in a mug cake recipe by a tablespoon. It's a great flour for muffins, crumbles, spice cakes, etc.

In a large bowl, mix together 4½ cups brown rice flour, 2 cups sweet rice flour, 1 cup oat flour, 1 cup almond flour, ½ cup arrowroot flour, 2 tablespoons xanthan gum, 2 tablespoons gluten-free baking powder, and 1 teaspoon kosher salt.

Store in an airtight container. Mix well before each use.

## GLUTEN-FREE, SELF-RISING FLOUR MIX #4

Makes 6¼ cups / Prep time: 5 minutes

This is another light, bland mix that is good for almost any cake.

In a large bowl, mix together 4 cups white rice flour, 1¼ cups potato starch, ¾ cup tapioca flour, 3 teaspoons xanthan gum, 3 tablespoons baking powder, and 2 teaspoons kosher salt.

Store in an airtight container. Mix well before each use.

## NUT-FREE

Nuts can be omitted from any recipe without substitution to accommodate any nut allergies. But if you want to maintain the texture and crunch of the nuts, here are a few possibilities:

* Sunflower seeds or pumpkin seeds give a similar rich texture and crunch to nuts.

* Sunflower butter or soy butter can be used instead of peanut butter.

* Tahini is a butter made from sesame seeds that has a unique, slightly smoky flavor.

* Dried fruit or chocolate chips can add texture.

* Textured vegetable protein granules can be folded into the batter just before baking to give added texture. Just don't put too many in because they will soak up the moisture.

## VEGAN

You can make any of the mug cake recipes vegan by using one of the nondairy milk substitutes and a nondairy butter substitute previously mentioned. Any egg called for in the recipes can be handled in one of two ways:

1. Try leaving the egg out entirely. You may find that the texture is not that much different.

2. 1 tablespoon ground flaxseed mixed with 3 tablespoons water per egg called for in the recipe.

Chocolate chips and other added ingredients should be substituted with their vegan counterparts. Some vegans eat honey and some do not, so be sensitive to the possibilities if you're cooking for a vegan friend.

## LOW-CARB

It's always difficult to find treats and desserts for a low-carb diet. You can make mug cakes lower carb by making the following substitutions:

* Use almond flour or a commercially produced low-carb flour for the wheat-based flour called for in the recipe. You also can use 2 parts almond flour to 1 part coconut flour.

* Be aware that when you are using coconut flour, you may need to allow the cake to bake longer. Coconut soaks up moisture and the cake cooks differently than it does with regular flour.

* Use a sugar substitute.

* Use heavy cream or coconut milk for the milk called for. You can even use half cream and half coconut milk to save some calories.

* Make sure any additional ingredients the recipes calls for are low-carb.

* Whipped cream or sour cream sweetened with a little stevia or another sugar-free sweetener makes a perfect low-carb topping for low-carb cakes.

## Make Your Own Mug Cake

Mug cakes are very simple, consisting of just six basic ingredients: flour, butter, sugar, eggs, liquid, and salt. Once you have that formula down, you can create your own signature mug cake anytime you want. Experiment with flavors and added ingredients to create whatever combination seems interesting to you. The sky's the limit.

# BASIC

*Serves: 2  Prep time: 2 minutes  Cook time: 5 minutes*

You can adjust this basic cake to suit your own tastes. Don't be afraid to add a bit more sugar if you like it sweeter. Want it just a little moister? Try shorter cooking times. You can also add a few drops of vanilla or other extract flavors to enhance the cake flavor.

¼ cup unsalted butter, melted

¼ cup sugar

¼ cup milk

1 egg

½ cup self-rising flour

1. In a medium bowl, mix together the butter, sugar, milk, and egg until very smooth.

2. Add the flour, and mix *just* until well blended and smooth.

3. Divide the batter between 2 mugs, being careful not to fill the mugs more than half full.

4. Microwave each cake for 1½ to 2½ minutes on high, or until the top is firm but springy when lightly touched, and serve.

# BASIC CHOCOLATE

*Serves: 2  Prep time: 2 minutes  Cook time: 5 minutes*

You can never go wrong with a little chocolate cake. Just like the basic mug cake recipe, you can customize this to your own tastes. Add a dash of cayenne pepper to spice things up or a sprinkle of instant coffee crystals for an unexpected kick. The possibilities are as endless as your imagination, and you're sure to find many treasured variations of this cake.

| | |
|---|---|
| ¼ cup unsalted butter, melted | ¼ cup self-rising flour |
| ½ cup sugar | ¼ cup cocoa (extra-dark works best) |
| ¼ cup milk | Pinch kosher salt |
| 1 egg | |

1. In a medium bowl, mix together the butter, sugar, milk, and egg until very smooth.

2. Add the flour, cocoa, and salt, mixing *just* until blended.

3. Divide the batter between 2 mugs, being careful not to fill the mugs more than half full.

4. Microwave each cake for 1½ to 2½ minutes on high, or until the top is firm but springy when lightly touched, and serve.

You see? You need very little to make a basic white or chocolate mug cake. Now that you have the essential ingredients down, it doesn't take much to create your own delicious variations. Keep in mind that you are working with small amounts of batter, so you will need to be careful not to put too many additional ingredients in the cake. Generally speaking, a total of 3 to 4 tablespoons of an added ingredient is plenty. So you could add 1 tablespoon of nuts and 3 tablespoons of mini chocolate chips, for example, giving you a total of 4 tablespoons. Adding 2 tablespoons of blueberries and 2 tablespoons of chopped strawberries also meets the 4 tablespoon maximum. More than that will weigh the cake down.

Here are a few addition suggestions to get those creative juices flowing:

* Add ¼ teaspoon of flavoring such as vanilla extract, maple, orange, lemon, or mint.

* Add ½ teaspoon ground cinnamon, ginger, cloves, cardamom, nutmeg, or a mixture of ground spices.

* Substitute 1 tablespoon rum, bourbon, or liqueur for 1 tablespoon of the milk.

* Use cold black coffee in place of the milk.

* Use juice in place of the milk.

* Add 3 tablespoons mini chocolate chips.

* Add 3 tablespoons mini candy-coated chocolates.

* Add 3 tablespoons chopped nuts.

* Add 3 tablespoons dried cherries, raisins, cranberries, or other dried fruit, chopped if needed (if the fruit is too large, it will all sink to the bottom of the cake).

* Add ¼ cup blueberries, raspberries, or other fresh berries.

* Add ¼ cup chopped apple, pear, or pineapple.

* Add 2 tablespoons pumpkin purée, applesauce, or another fruit purée.

* Add 3 tablespoons chopped peanut butter cups.

# DRESS IT UP

There are times when you'll want to make a quick mug cake and eat it just as soon as it has cooled down. Other times you'll want to dress up your favorite mug cake, whether it's because you are having company or because you need a little self-nurturing. Luckily, dressing up a mug cake is just about as easy as making one.

ADDING A DOLLOP OF FLUFFY WHIPPED CREAM is a simple, beautiful way to make your mug cake look a little fancy. Dress it up even further by sprinkling grated chocolate on top of the whipped cream. It's easy to do—just run a milk chocolate bar across the small holes of a grater. You can do the same with white chocolate.

BUTTERCREAM FROSTING is another possibility. Once you've spooned frosting on top of your cooled mug cake, dress it up even more by adding colorful sprinkles or fresh fruit.

HOW ABOUT TOASTED MARSHMALLOW? Take the cake out of the microwave just before it's done and add a marshmallow or two to the top. Continue cooking it in the microwave until the cake is done and the marshmallow is melted and gooey. That's going to be hard to resist!

FRUIT TOPPING is a classic way to make any cake special. A spoonful or two of cherry or blueberry pie filling makes an easy and delicious topping.

Mix it up even more by combining ingredients, keeping in mind the 3-to-4 tablespoon rule. Some great combinations include:

* Coffee liqueur and chocolate chips

* Chopped white chocolate and raspberries

* Coffee, chocolate chips, and pecans

* Banana, pecans, and spices

* Bourbon and pumpkin

* Cranberry, orange zest, and walnuts

What are some of your favorite flavor combinations? Give it a try and find out.

# 3

# *The Classics*

Vanilla Mug Cake *33*

Spice Mug Cake *34*

Caramel Mug Cake *35*

Devil's Food Mug Cake *36*

Lemon Mug Cake *37*

Marble Mug Cake *38*

Yellow Mug Cake *39*

Carrot Cake in a Mug *40*

Pineapple Upside-Down Mug Cake *41*

Pound Cake in a Mug *43*

# TRANSFORM YOUR MUG CAKE

A mug cake is a quick and easy dessert on its own, but if you stop there you'll be missing out on one of the best things about these delicious little cakes: They can be used as the starting point for a variety of desserts. If it starts with a cake as a base, you can make it a mug cake. Consider the following possibilities:

Fruit shortcakes • Tortes • Ice cream sundaes • Banana splits

One of the most iconic of American desserts is the banana split. You can improve on that classic even more by using slices of banana mug cake as the base and building it up from there.

## CLASSIC BANANA SPLIT

*Makes 2  Prep time: 10 minutes*

2 Banana Mug Cakes (see page 63)

2 ripe bananas, sliced

2 scoops vanilla ice cream, divided

2 scoops chocolate ice cream, divided

2 scoops strawberry ice cream, divided

2 tablespoons caramel syrup, divided

2 tablespoons hot fudge syrup, divided

¼ cup sliced strawberries, divided

2 tablespoons strawberry syrup, divided

¼ cup whipped cream, divided

2 tablespoons chopped pecans, divided

2 maraschino cherries

1. Slice each cake horizontally into 3 rounds.

2. In each of 2 banana split dishes or bowls, overlap 3 cake rounds.

3. Cover the cake rounds in each dish with half of the sliced bananas.

4. In each dish, place 1 scoop each of vanilla, chocolate, and strawberry ice cream on top of the banana slices.

5. In each dish, cover the vanilla ice cream with 1 tablespoon of caramel syrup and the chocolate ice cream with 1 tablespoon of hot fudge. Cover the strawberry ice cream in each dish with ⅛ cup of the sliced strawberries and 1 tablespoon of the strawberry syrup.

6. Cover each concoction with whipped cream, and top with pecans and a cherry.

# VANILLA

## MUG CAKE

*Serves: 2  **Prep time:** 2 minutes  **Cook time:** 3 minutes*

Nothing is more classic than vanilla. Vanilla actually comes from the vanilla orchid, the only orchid that bears fruit. The flavoring is made from the seedpod of this plant. Natural vanilla extract has a much better flavor than imitation vanilla and is worth paying a little more for. Try different brands and types of the flavoring to see what you like best. All vanilla is not the same.

| | |
|---|---|
| ½ cup self-rising flour | ½ cup milk |
| ¼ cup sugar | 1 teaspoon vanilla extract |
| Pinch salt | 3 tablespoons unsalted butter, melted |

1. In a medium bowl, whisk together the flour, sugar, and salt.

2. Add the milk, vanilla, and butter to the dry ingredients, mixing just until combined.

3. Divide the batter between 2 mugs, being careful not to fill the mugs more than halfway.

4. Microwave each cake for 1½ minutes, or until the top is firm but springy when touched, and serve.

*Topping Suggestion:* A scoop of chocolate ice cream is the perfect accompaniment to warm vanilla cake. If you prefer something less rich, try warm apple pie filling. If you want to really indulge, treat yourself to a spoonful of each.

*Make It Gluten-Free:* Swap any gluten-free flour plus ⅛ teaspoon baking powder for the self-rising flour.

*Variation:* Push a caramel candy into the center of the batter before cooking. When eaten warm, the luscious cake will have a gooey filling. If you like salted caramel, sprinkle a little sea salt over the top of the cake.

# SPICE

*Serves: 2  **Prep time:** 2 minutes  **Cook time:** 3 minutes*

A spice cake is the perfect antidote to chilly weather. Added bonus: It makes the house smell good and provides the family with a quick little treat. Cinnamon, cloves, and ginger are the traditional spice cake flavorings, but try adding a little ground cardamom for a citrusy boost. This is a great cake to make in a jelly jar and send in a school lunch. Wrap it in aluminum foil so it stays warm.

| | |
|---|---|
| ½ cup self-rising flour | Pinch salt |
| ¼ cup sugar | ½ cup milk |
| Pinch ground cinnamon | ½ teaspoon vanilla extract |
| Pinch ground cloves | 3 tablespoons unsalted butter, melted |
| Pinch ground ginger | |

1.  In a medium bowl, whisk together the flour, sugar, cinnamon, cloves, ginger, and salt.

2.  Add the milk, vanilla, and butter to the dry ingredients, mixing just until combined.

3.  Divide the batter between 2 mugs, being careful not to fill the mugs more than halfway.

4.  Microwave each mug for 1½ minutes, or until the top is firm but springy when lightly touched, and serve.

    *Topping Suggestion:* Spice cake is especially good with a Cream Cheese Frosting (page 158) but other topping possibilities include Salted Caramel Sauce (page 165), Maple Frosting (page 161), and Vanilla Glaze (page 171).

    *Variation:* Fold 3 tablespoons finely chopped walnuts into the batter before baking for additional texture and a little crunch.

# CARAMEL
## MUG CAKE

*Serves: 2  **Prep time:** 2 minutes  **Cook time:** 3 minutes*

Caramel is one of those old-fashioned flavors everyone loves. Buttery and sweet, caramel cake gets its flavor from brown sugar. Try experimenting with both golden (sometimes called "light") brown sugar and dark brown sugar to see which you prefer. The golden brown sugar gives a much more subtle flavor. Sprinkle the top with some caramel corn for an unexpected crunch.

| | |
|---|---|
| ½ cup self-rising flour | ¼ cup milk |
| ¼ cup brown sugar | ½ teaspoon vanilla extract |
| Pinch salt | 3 tablespoons unsalted butter, melted |
| 1 egg | |

1.  In a medium bowl, whisk together the flour, brown sugar, and salt.

2.  Add the egg, milk, vanilla, and butter to the dry ingredients, mixing *just* until combined.

3.  Divide the batter between 2 mugs, being careful not to fill the mugs more than half full.

4.  Microwave each mug for 1½ minutes, or until the top is firm but springy when touched, and serve.

*Topping Suggestion:* A scoop of vanilla ice cream is the perfect accompaniment to warm caramel cake. If you prefer something less rich, try warm apple pie filling. If you want to really indulge, treat yourself to a spoonful of each.

*Make It Gluten-Free:* Swap any gluten-free flour plus ⅛ teaspoon baking powder for the self-rising flour.

# DEVIL'S FOOD

MUG CAKE

*Serves: 2  Prep time: 2 minutes  Cook time: 3 minutes*

Chocolate is incredibly popular, and the variations seem endless. Devil's food cake is different from chocolate cake because it uses buttermilk and dark chocolate to achieve its deep color and flavor. Because this recipe includes baking powder and baking soda, we won't use self-rising flour.

⅓ cup cake flour

⅓ cup sugar

3 tablespoons extra-dark cocoa powder

¼ teaspoon baking powder

⅛ teaspoon baking soda

1 egg, beaten

⅓ cup buttermilk

⅓ cup lightly flavored oil, such as peanut or vegetable oil

¼ teaspoon vanilla extract

Pinch salt

1. In a medium bowl, mix together the flour, sugar, cocoa powder, baking powder, baking soda, egg, buttermilk, oil, vanilla, and salt *just* until smooth.

2. Divide the batter between 2 mugs, being careful not to fill the mugs more than half full.

3. Microwave each mug for 1½ minutes, or until the top is firm but springy when touched, and serve.

*Topping Suggestion:* Chocolate Ganache (page 162) is the perfect creamy, chocolatey topping for this rich, dark cake.

*Variation:* Fold ¼ cup mini chocolate chips into the batter before cooking for a chocolate chocolate-chip cake that is moist and gooey.

# LEMON

*Serves: 2  Prep time: 2 minutes  Cook time: 2 minutes*

This lemon cake is light and moist—perfect for a quick snack on a warm afternoon. The lemon should be just tangy enough to get your taste buds anticipating the next bite. Experiment a little and adjust the sugar up or down to get the exact lemon flavor you crave. Make it special by crushing hard lemon candies and sprinkling them on top before serving.

½ cup self-rising flour

⅓ cup milk

⅓ cup sugar

2 tablespoons vegetable oil

2 tablespoons freshly squeezed lemon juice

Zest of 1 lemon

1. In a medium bowl, mix together the flour, milk, sugar, oil, and lemon juice.

2. Stir in the lemon zest until the batter is *just* smooth.

3. Divide the batter between 2 mugs, being careful not to fill the mugs more than halfway.

4. Microwave each mug for about 1 minute, or until the top is firm but springy when touched, and serve.

*Topping Suggestion:* Lemon Glaze (page 169) or Vanilla Glaze (page 171), Lemon Curd (page 166), or a dollop of whipped cream would be perfect on this light, tangy cake.

*Make It Vegan:* Substitute rice or almond milk for the milk.

*Variation:* Fold ¼ cup poppy seeds into the batter for a lemon–poppy seed cake.

# MARBLE

*Serves: 2  **Prep time:** 2 minutes  **Cook time:** 3 minutes*

Why decide between chocolate and vanilla cake when you can have both? Kids will have fun alternating spoonfuls of chocolate and vanilla batter into their mug. Then it's a simple matter to drag a knife through the batter to make the swirls. It couldn't be easier—or more delicious.

| | |
|---|---|
| ½ cup self-rising flour | 1 teaspoon vanilla extract |
| ½ cup sugar | 3 tablespoons unsalted butter, melted |
| Pinch salt | 1 tablespoon cocoa |
| ½ cup milk | |

1. In a medium bowl, whisk together the flour, sugar, and salt.

2. Add the milk, vanilla, and butter to the dry ingredients, and mix *just* until combined.

3. In a small, clean bowl, stir half the batter together with the cocoa until well combined.

4. Add a spoonful of vanilla batter to each mug, followed by a spoonful of chocolate batter. Continue adding alternate spoonfuls of batter until the mugs are half full.

5. Run a knife through the batter in each mug to swirl the cake batters together and create the marble effect.

6. Microwave each mug for 1½ minutes, or until the top is firm but springy when lightly touched, and serve.

*Topping Suggestion:* Chocolate Frosting (page 159) or hot fudge sauce is a great way to finish off this cake. If you have a few extra minutes, swirl both Chocolate and Vanilla Frosting (page 157) onto the top to go with the marble cake theme.

*Variation:* Fold 1 tablespoon freshly grated orange zest into the vanilla cake batter for a fresh citrus taste.

# YELLOW

*Serves:* 2  **Prep time:** *2 minutes*  **Cook time:** *5 minutes*

A yellow cake is golden and buttery with a touch of vanilla. It achieves its classic flavor and velvety texture by using egg yolks in the batter rather than whole eggs. The egg yolks add the richness that gives this cake its luxurious texture. A bit wary about separating the yolk from the egg white? Here's a tip: Eggs are much easier to separate when they are at room temperature.

¼ cup unsalted butter, melted

¼ cup plus 1 tablespoon sugar

¼ cup milk

2 egg yolks

½ teaspoon vanilla

½ cup self-rising flour

Pinch kosher salt

1. In a medium bowl, mix together the butter and sugar until smooth.

2. Add in the milk, egg yolks, and vanilla and beat until well mixed.

3. Add the flour and salt, stirring *just* until smooth.

4. Divide the batter between 2 mugs, being careful not to fill the mugs more than half full.

5. Microwave each mug for $1\frac{1}{2}$ to $2\frac{1}{2}$ minutes, or until the top is firm but springy when lightly touched, and serve.

*Topping Suggestion:* Chocolate Frosting (page 159) with sprinkles is a classic topping for yellow cake, or try something a bit different and spoon your favorite fruit pie filling over the top.

*Make It Sugar-Free:* Use xylitol, erythritol, or your favorite sugar substitute instead of the sugar.

*Variation:* Fold 3 tablespoons chopped chocolate toffee into the batter for an unexpected crunch.

# CARROT CAKE
IN A MUG

*Serves: 2  Prep time: 2 minutes  Cook time: 5 minutes*

Even vegetable-resistant children will love this warm, spicy carrot cake. For even more flavor, buy whole nutmeg and grate it yourself. It's easy to do, and the flavor is indescribable. This recipe will make your whole kitchen smell like the winter holidays.

¼ cup coconut oil, melted

¼ cup sugar

1 tablespoon brown sugar

¼ teaspoon ground cinnamon

Pinch kosher salt

2 tablespoons milk

2 tablespoons pineapple juice

1 egg

½ teaspoon vanilla

½ cup self-rising flour

¼ teaspoon ground nutmeg

¼ cup grated carrot

¼ cup chopped walnuts

1. In a medium bowl, mix together the coconut oil, sugar, brown sugar, cinnamon, and salt. Stir until smooth.

2. Add the milk, pineapple juice, egg, and vanilla, and beat until well mixed.

3. Add the flour and nutmeg, stirring *just* until smooth.

4. Fold the carrots and walnuts into the batter.

5. Divide the batter between 2 mugs, being careful not to fill the mugs more than halfway.

6. Microwave each mug for 1½ to 2½ minutes, or until the top is firm but springy when lightly touched, and serve.

*Topping Suggestion:* Cream Cheese Frosting (page 158) is a classic topping with carrot cake. If you prefer something else, whipped cream or vanilla ice cream is good, too.

*Variation:* Fold 2 tablespoons chopped raisins into the batter for extra sweetness and nutrition.

# PINEAPPLE UPSIDE-DOWN
## MUG CAKE

*Serves: 2  Prep time: 2 minutes  Cook time: 3 minutes*

Go retro with pineapple upside-down mug cake. The pineapple combines with the butter and brown sugar in the bottom of the dish to make some sort of magic that will have you licking the dish clean. This mug cake is microwaved in two parts, but don't let that deter you. It's worth it. The sugar syrup gets very hot, so it's not a good choice for young aspiring cooks. Leave this one to the older kids.

FOR THE TOPPING

⅓ cup dark brown sugar

2 teaspoons unsweetened
   pineapple juice

2 pineapple rings

1 maraschino cherry, halved

1 tablespoon chopped nuts

FOR THE CAKE

½ cup flour

¼ cup sugar

1 egg

2 tablespoons unsalted butter, melted

¼ cup unsweetened pineapple juice

TO MAKE THE TOPPING

1. Grease 2 mugs with butter.

2. Mix the dark brown sugar and pineapple juice in the bottom of a mug. Transfer half the mixture to the second mug.

3. Add a pineapple ring to each of the mugs and put half the cherry in the center of each ring. Sprinkle each with 1½ teaspoons of nuts.

4. Microwave each mug for 30 seconds, or until the mixture is bubbly and turns syrupy.

TO MAKE THE CAKE

1. In a medium bowl, mix together the flour and sugar.

2. Add the egg, melted butter, and pineapple juice to the dry ingredients, stirring *just* until smooth.

3. Divide the batter between the 2 mugs, on top of the syrupy pineapple ring, cherry, and nuts, being careful not to fill the mugs more than halfway.

*Continued*

4. Microwave each mug for 1 minute, or until the top is firm but springy when lightly touched.

5. Let each cake cool in its mug for about 3 minutes, and then turn it out onto a plate. The bottom of the cake now becomes the top.

*Topping Suggestion:* Pineapple upside-down cake doesn't need a topping since it makes its own, but a scoop of vanilla ice cream or a spoonful of whipped cream is wonderful with it.

*Substitution Tip:* Make this dairy-free by using coconut oil instead of butter. You can leave the nuts out entirely if you wish.

*Variation:* Substitute 1 tablespoon rum for 1 tablespoon pineapple juice for an added depth of flavor.

# POUND CAKE
## IN A MUG

*Serves: 2  Prep time: 2 minutes  Cook time: 4 minutes*

Pound cake is dense, yet buttery and tender, which makes it the perfect vehicle for fresh fruit, a scoop of ice cream, or a lavish pour of your favorite dessert sauce. The traditional oven-baked pound cake has a dark side: It takes forever to bake. Well, no more. This mug pound cake can be enjoyed in less than 5 minutes. It's a great base for strawberry shortcake. Just add ice cream and berries.

½ cup self-rising flour

3 tablespoons almond flour

½ cup sugar

2 egg yolks

1 teaspoon vanilla

¼ cup unsalted butter, melted

¼ cup heavy cream

1. In a medium bowl, mix together the self-rising flour, almond flour, and sugar.

2. Add the egg yolks, vanilla, butter, and cream, stirring *just* until well blended.

3. Divide the batter between 2 mugs, being careful not to fill the mugs more than halfway.

4. Microwave each mug for 1½ to 2 minutes, or until the top is firm but springy when lightly touched, and serve.

*Topping Suggestion:* A sprinkle of confectioners' sugar or a dollop of whipped cream is all that is needed on this velvety pound cake.

*Variation:* Use brown sugar in place of white sugar and fold in ¼ cup finely chopped pecans for a Southern-style pecan pound cake.

# 4

·············

# *Chocolate, Chocolate Everywhere*

Lava Mug Cake *47*

Gooey Chocolate Mug Cake *48*

Mexican Chocolate Mug Cake *49*

Chocolate-Pecan Mug Cake *50*

German Chocolate Mug Cake *51*

Chocolate-Peanut Butter Mug Cake *52*

Chocolate–Mint Mug Cake *53*

Holy Cow! Mug Cake *54*

# WHY HAVE A LITTLE CHOCOLATE WHEN YOU CAN HAVE A LOT?

Chocolate mug cakes are perfect on their own—there is nothing richer or more luxurious. But is there such a thing as too much chocolate? Of course not. These delicious homemade chocolate chips will take any of the chocolate mug cakes in this chapter to new heights. The best part: Making your own chocolate chips allows you to control the sweetness as well as the ingredients that go into them. Use the sugar or sugar-free sweetener of your choice. Cut the chocolate small for chips, or leave them in larger pieces for chocolate chunks. Because of the simplicity of the ingredients in homemade chocolate chips, they will melt much more quickly than commercial chocolate chips. The added bonus: They're vegan.

## HOMEMADE VEGAN COCOA CHIPS OR CHUNKS

*Makes 3 cups* **Prep time:** *10 minutes, plus 20 to 45 minutes for chilling*
**Cook time:** *2 minutes*

1 cup cocoa butter or coconut oil

1 cup cocoa

¼ to ⅓ cup sweetener, sugar, or xylitol

½ teaspoon chocolate extract

1 teaspoon vanilla extract

1. In a small pot over medium heat, melt the cocoa butter.

2. Transfer the melted butter to a medium bowl or a blender.

3. Add the cocoa, sweetener and chocolate and vanilla extracts to the butter; mix well.

4. Pour the mixture into a lightly greased, 8-by-8-inch baking dish. Chill in the refrigerator for at least 45 minutes until completely hardened.

5. Using a knife or spatula, break large pieces of the chocolate out of the pan and place them on a cutting board.

6. Using a sharp knife, chop the chocolate to the desired size. Store the chips in a tightly sealed container in a cool place, the refrigerator, or the freezer.

# LAVA

*Serves: 2  Prep time: 2 minutes  Cook time: 1 minute*

The perfect lava cake is a moist, dense chocolate cake with a molten pool of chocolate ganache in the center. Eyes of every age will light up when that chocolatey pool spills out as the cake is opened up. The trick is not to overbake these little guys.

| | |
|---|---|
| 3 tablespoons unsalted butter, melted | 2 tablespoons cocoa |
| ¼ cup milk | Pinch salt |
| ¼ cup sugar | 1-ounce square milk or dark chocolate, cut in half |
| ¼ cup self-rising flour | |

1. In a medium bowl, whisk together the butter, milk, and sugar until smooth.

2. Add the flour, cocoa, and salt, stirring *just* until smooth.

3. Divide the batter between 2 mugs, being careful not to fill the mugs more than half full.

4. Push a chocolate square half into each mug, making sure that the chocolate is completely covered with batter.

5. Microwave each mug for 30 seconds. The cake is done if it has risen and the top looks done. It may be slightly sticky to the touch. Eat immediately.

*Topping Suggestion:* All you really need with this is a scoop of your favorite ice cream. Take things up a notch by sprinkling chopped white chocolate onto the mug cake just before serving.

*Variation:* Use a peanut butter cup in place of the milk chocolate. The creaminess of the peanut butter lends a different texture to the lava mug cake.

# GOOEY CHOCOLATE
## MUG CAKE

*Serves: 2  Prep time: 2 minutes  Cook time: 2 minutes, 3 minutes resting*

What better way to turn a bad day into a good one? While the lava cake has a pool of warm chocolate in its center, this gooey mug cake has random puddles of chocolate throughout. It's unpredictable and messy but very, very addicting.

¼ cup self-rising flour

¼ cup sugar

¼ cup cocoa powder

Pinch salt

¼ cup milk

¼ cup unsalted butter, melted

2 eggs, beaten

1 teaspoon vanilla

⅓ cup milk chocolate chips

1. In a medium bowl, whisk together the flour, sugar, cocoa powder, and salt.

2. Add the milk, butter, eggs, and vanilla to the dry ingredients, stirring *just* until smooth.

3. Fold the chocolate chips into the batter.

4. Divide the batter between the 2 mugs, being careful not to fill the mugs more than half full.

5. Microwave each cake for about 1 minute, being careful not to overcook.

6. Let the mug cakes cool for about 3 minutes. Eat while still warm and gooey.

*Topping Suggestion:* Hot fudge and Salted Caramel Sauce (page 165) are both delicious additions. In fact, why not use both at the same time?

*Make It Gluten-Free:* Use your favorite gluten-free flour and ⅛ teaspoon baking powder in place of the self-rising flour.

*Variation:* For a personalized treat, use your favorite candy bar, chopped, instead of the chocolate chips.

# MEXICAN CHOCOLATE
## MUG CAKE

*Serves: 2  **Prep time:** 2 minutes  **Cook time:** 4 minutes*

Chocolate was discovered by the Aztecs and reserved for only the most important people in society. Mexican chocolate is a dark chocolate, often with cinnamon added. This recipe gives a nod to the origins of chocolate by adding both cinnamon and just a touch of chipotle for a smoky bite. It's a great way to introduce younger kids to more complex flavors.

¼ cup unsalted butter, melted

¼ cup sugar

2 tablespoons brown sugar

1 egg

¼ cup milk

¼ cup self-rising flour

¼ cup cocoa (extra-dark cocoa works best)

½ teaspoon ground cinnamon

¼ teaspoon chipotle powder

Pinch kosher salt

1.  In a large measuring cup or medium bowl, mix together the butter, sugar, and brown sugar until smooth. Add in the egg and milk and beat until well mixed.

2.  Add the flour, cocoa, cinnamon, chipotle powder, and salt, stirring *just* until smooth.

3.  Divide the batter between 2 mugs, being careful not to fill the mugs more than half full.

4.  Microwave each mug for 1 to 2 minutes, or until the top is firm but springy when lightly touched, and serve.

*Topping Suggestions:* Top with Chocolate Frosting (page 159), Chocolate Ganache (page 162), or just a sprinkle of confectioners' sugar.

*Variation:* Fold ¼ cup bittersweet chocolate chips into the batter for an extra chocolate kick.

# CHOCOLATE-PECAN

### MUG CAKE

*Serves: 2  Prep time: 2 minutes  Cook time: 4 minutes*

Chocolate and pecans go well together in everything from brownies to ice cream. Here the cake is moist and velvety, and the crunch of pecans combines with it for a winning texture. You'll get even more flavor from the pecans—most nuts really—if you'll toast them in a 350°F oven for about 5 minutes.

¼ cup unsalted butter, melted

¼ cup sugar

1 egg

¼ cup milk

¼ cup self-rising flour

¼ cup cocoa (extra-dark cocoa works best)

Pinch salt

¼ cup chopped pecans

1. In a large measuring cup or medium bowl, mix together the butter and sugar until smooth.

2. Add in the egg and milk, and beat until well mixed.

3. Add the flour, cocoa, and salt, stirring *just* until smooth.

4. Divide the batter between 2 mugs, being careful not to fill the mugs more than half full.

5. Microwave each mug for 1 to 2 minutes, until the top is firm but springy when lightly touched, and serve.

*Topping Suggestion:* Chocolate Frosting (page 159) or Chocolate Ganache (page 162) are classic toppings, but the Bourbon Caramel Syrup (page 163) is out of this world.

*Make It Nut-Free:* Substitute shelled sunflower seeds or candy-coated chocolate pieces for the pecans.

*Variation:* Just about any type of nut can be used in this cake. Try it with almonds or walnuts instead of the pecans.

# GERMAN CHOCOLATE
## MUG CAKE

*Serves:* 2  *Prep time:* 5 *minutes*  *Cook time:* 4 *minutes, 3 minutes resting*

German chocolate cake is not named after Germany or anything related to the country. It is actually named for Sam German, who developed the chocolate in 1852. The cake made its first appearance in a Dallas newspaper nearly a hundred years later. If anyone dislikes the texture of coconut, leave it out and add a few more pecans.

¼ cup unsalted butter, melted

¼ cup sugar

1 egg

2 ounces German's Sweet Chocolate, melted

¼ cup milk

½ cup self-rising flour

2 tablespoons shredded, sweetened coconut, divided

¼ cup chopped pecans, divided

2 tablespoons Salted Caramel Sauce (page 165), divided

1. Grease each mug with butter.

2. In a large measuring cup or medium bowl, mix together the butter and sugar with a fork until smooth. Add in the egg, chocolate, and milk and beat until well mixed.

3. Add the flour, stirring *just* until smooth.

4. Add 1 tablespoon of coconut to each mug, followed by ⅛ cup pecans and 1 tablespoon Salted Caramel Sauce each.

5. Divide the cake batter between the mugs, being careful not to fill the mugs more than half full.

6. Microwave each cake for 1 to 2 minutes, or until the top is firm but springy when lightly touched.

7. Let each cake cool for 2 or 3 minutes, turn out onto a plate, and serve.

*Topping Suggestion:* This mug cake makes its own topping, but adding a scoop of chocolate ice cream makes it an extra-special treat.

*Variation:* To make a turtle mug cake, omit the coconut and add two more tablespoons of pecans.

# CHOCOLATE-PEANUT BUTTER
## MUG CAKE

*Serves: 2  Prep time: 2 minutes  Cook time: 4 minutes*

You just can't go wrong with peanut butter and chocolate. This cake is dark and moist with a peanut butter cup tucked inside. When the cake is warm, the peanut butter cup becomes a delicious, gooey surprise that enhances the peanut butter flavor in the cake itself. The requests for this mug cake will be often and very loud.

3 tablespoons peanut butter

1 tablespoon vegetable or peanut oil

¼ cup sugar

1 egg

¼ cup milk

¼ cup self-rising flour

¼ cup cocoa (extra-dark cocoa works best)

2 peanut butter cups

1. In a large measuring cup or medium bowl, mix the peanut butter, oil, and sugar with a fork until smooth. Add in the egg and milk, and beat until well mixed.

2. Add the flour and cocoa, stirring *just* until smooth.

3. Divide the batter between 2 mugs, being careful not to fill the mugs more than half full.

4. Push a peanut butter cup into the batter in each mug, making sure it is completely covered by the batter.

5. Microwave each mug for 1 to 2 minutes on high, or until the top is firm but springy when lightly touched, and serve.

*Topping Suggestion:* Hot fudge, Chocolate Frosting (page 159), or Chocolate Ganache (page 162) are excellent on this cake. Think about adding a scoop of peanut butter cup ice cream on the side. Who doesn't love that?

*Make It Dairy-Free:* Use almond milk in place of the milk.

*Variation:* Fold 2 tablespoons peanut butter chips into the batter for even more peanut butter goodness.

# CHOCOLATE-MINT
## MUG CAKE

*Serves: 2* **Prep time:** *2 minutes* **Cook time:** *4 minutes*

Grasshoppers. Thin mint cookies. The chocolate and mint combinations list can go on and on—it's a pairing made in heaven. This cake is rich and chocolatey with that refreshing mint aftertaste that keeps you going back for more. The grown-ups in your house will surely enjoy 1 tablespoon crème de menthe or peppermint schnapps in place of the mint extract. Just cut back on the milk by 1 tablespoon to keep the proportions right.

| | |
|---|---|
| 4 tablespoons unsalted butter, melted | ½ teaspoon mint extract |
| ¼ cup sugar | ¼ cup self-rising flour |
| ¼ cup milk | ¼ cup cocoa (extra-dark cocoa works best) |
| 1 egg | |

1. In a large measuring cup or medium bowl, mix together the butter and sugar with a fork until smooth. Add in the milk, egg, and mint extract, and beat until well mixed.

2. Add the flour and cocoa, stirring *just* until smooth.

3. Divide the batter between 2 mugs, being careful not to fill the mugs more than half full.

4. Microwave each mug for 1 to 2 minutes on high, or until the top is firm but springy when lightly touched, and serve.

   *Topping Suggestion:* Hot fudge, Chocolate Frosting (page 159), or Chocolate Ganache (page 162) add more chocolate flavor to this moist cake. Enhance the mint flavor with crushed or chopped chocolate-covered, mint-flavored cookies or candies sprinkled on top of the mug cake.

   *Variation:* If you want to make this mug cake even mintier, chop some chocolate-covered after-dinner mints and fold them into the batter before microwaving to create pockets of melty chocolate mint in the cake.

# HOLY COW!
## MUG CAKE

*Serves: 2  **Prep time:** 2 minutes  **Cook time:** 4 minutes, 5 minutes soaking*

What makes a Holy Cow cake? A cake so rich and so good that when you bite into it, you'll exclaim, "Holy Cow!" This rich chocolate cake has chopped Butterfinger candy bars folded into the batter. And as if that weren't enough, the cake is soaked with caramel and sweetened condensed milk after baking. If this mug cake doesn't take care of that sweet craving, nothing will.

4 tablespoons unsalted butter, melted

¼ cup sugar

1 egg

½ teaspoon vanilla extract

¼ cup milk

½ cup self-rising flour

¼ cup cocoa (extra-dark cocoa works best)

¼ cup chopped Butterfinger candy bars

2 tablespoons Salted Caramel Sauce (page 165), divided

2 tablespoons sweetened condensed milk, divided

1. In a large measuring cup or medium bowl, mix the butter and sugar until smooth. Add the egg, vanilla, and milk to the bowl, and beat until well mixed.

2. Add the flour and cocoa, stirring *just* until smooth.

3. Fold the candy into the batter.

4. Divide the batter between 2 mugs, being careful not to fill the mugs more than half full.

5. Microwave each mug for 1 to 2 minutes, or until the top is firm but springy when lightly touched.

6. As soon each mug cake comes out of the microwave, poke holes in the top of the cake with a knife or toothpick. Spoon 1 table-spoon of Salted Caramel Sauce (page 165) and 1 tablespoon of the sweetened condensed milk on top of each cake. Let the cakes soak for 5 minutes before eating.

*Topping Suggestion:* Whipped cream is the traditional way to top this rich cake. Add some grated chocolate for good measure.

*Make It Gluten-Free:* Use your preferred gluten-free flour or almond flour in place of the self-rising flour. Be sure to add ⅛ teaspoon baking powder. The sauce and condensed milk added to the finished cake helps keep it moist.

*Variation:* Use piña colada mix in place of the sweetened condensed milk for a tropical flair.

# 5

# *Get Fruity*

Strawberry Shortcake in a Mug *59*

Lemon-Blueberry Mug Cake *60*

Blueberry–White Chocolate Mug Cake *61*

Cherry–Chocolate Chip Mug Cake *62*

Banana Mug Cake *63*

Banana-Chocolate-Peanut-Butter Mug Cake *64*

Applesauce Mug Cake *65*

Key Lime Mug Cake *66*

White Chocolate–Raspberry Mug Cake *67*

# FRUIT PLUS CAKE EQUALS YUM

Using fresh fruit in season is the best way to add bright flavor to your mug cakes. Not only does it add a layer of flavor, but it adds a boost of vitamins, minerals, and fiber as well.

Seasonal fruits vary according to where you live, too. For example, strawberries are in season in April in Texas but not until June in Michigan. Use the following list as a guide, but double-check what is in season in your immediate locale.

## SPRING

* Apricots
* Grapefruit
* Honeydew
* Limes
* Mangos
* Oranges
* Rhubarb
* Strawberries
* Tangerines

## SUMMER

* Blackberries
* Blueberries
* Cantaloupe
* Cherries
* Figs
* Peaches
* Plums
* Raspberries
* Strawberries
* Watermelon

## FALL

* Apples
* Cranberries
* Dates
* Gooseberries
* Grapes
* Key Limes
* Pears
* Pineapple

## WINTER

* Clementines
* Dates
* Grapefruit
* Kiwi
* Mandarin Oranges
* Oranges
* Tangerines

## AVAILABLE ALL YEAR

Some fruits always have to be brought in from various locales far away, so they are basically available all year at the same level of quality. These include:

* Bananas
* Coconut
* Dried Fruit
* Lemons
* Limes
* Papaya

# STRAWBERRY SHORTCAKE
## IN A MUG

*Serves: 2  **Prep time:** 2 minutes  **Cook time:** 4 minutes, 5 minutes resting*

Nothing tastes more like summer than strawberry shortcake. Make this mug cake version in a large jelly jar, top with the berries, and add a screw-on lid to make these easily transportable for perfect summer picnics. Just bring the whipped cream along in a separate container in the cooler. Any other summer fruit works just as well with this cake.

| | |
|---|---|
| 2 tablespoons vegetable oil | 1 egg |
| ¼ cup sugar | ½ cup self-rising flour |
| ½ teaspoon vanilla extract | ½ cup sliced strawberries |
| ¼ cup milk | Whipped cream, for topping |

1. In a large measuring cup or medium bowl, mix together the oil, sugar, vanilla, and milk. Add in the egg and beat until well mixed.

2. Add the flour, stirring *just* until smooth.

3. Divide the batter between 2 mugs, being careful not to fill the mugs more than half full.

4. Microwave each mug for 1 to 2 minutes, or until the top is firm but springy when lightly touched, and serve.

5. Let each cake cool, about 5 minutes; then top each with ¼ cup of strawberries and a dollop of whipped cream and serve.

*Topping Suggestion:* You can substitute fat-free vanilla yogurt for the whipped cream to save some calories and still have a delicious dessert.

*Variation:* For a grown-up twist, use peaches in place of the strawberries and replace 1 tablespoon of milk with 1 tablespoon bourbon. Fold 1 tablespoon finely chopped pecans into the batter.

# LEMON-BLUEBERRY
## MUG CAKE

*Serves: 2  Prep time: 2 minutes  Cook time: 2 minutes*

Using oil instead of butter in this cake lets the fresh lemon flavor shine through. It's moist and tangy with a sweet burst of blueberry in every bite. Make this during blueberry season when blueberries are at their peak of flavor for best results—but feel free to use frozen blueberries if you just can't wait.

½ cup self-rising flour

⅓ cup milk

⅓ cup sugar

1 egg

2 tablespoons vegetable or peanut oil

2 tablespoons freshly squeezed lemon juice

Zest of 1 lemon

½ cup blueberries

1. In a medium bowl, mix together the flour, milk, sugar, egg, oil, and lemon juice.

2. Fold the lemon zest and blueberries into the batter.

3. Divide the batter between 2 mugs, being careful not to fill the mugs more than half full.

4. Microwave each cake for about 1 minute, or until the top is firm but springy when lightly touched, and serve.

*Topping Suggestion:* Lemon Glaze (page 169), Vanilla Glaze (page 171), Lemon Curd (page 166), or a dollop of whipped cream would be perfect on this summery dessert.

*Make It Vegan:* This cake can be made vegan by substituting almond milk for the milk and simply leaving out the egg.

*Variation:* Remove the cake from the mug when it has cooled a little (you'll need to grease the mug with butter before adding the batter so the cake comes out easily). Slice it into 4 layers. Add 1 layer back into the mug and top with Lemon Curd (page 166). Top the curd with the next layer of cake. Alternate cake layers and lemon curd until all the layers are used, ending with the last cake layer. Top that with a dollop of whipped cream and a few blueberries.

# BLUEBERRY-WHITE CHOCOLATE
## MUG CAKE

*Serves: 2  **Prep time:** 2 minutes  **Cook time:** 3 minutes*

Blueberries and white chocolate make for an unexpected combination in this sweet treat. The moist vanilla cake is studded with plump blueberries and rich, white chocolate chips. You can add 1 tablespoon chopped macadamia nuts if you like them, too. This is a quick cake that will bring some summer into the dreariest day.

| | |
|---|---|
| ½ cup self-rising flour | 2 tablespoons unsalted butter, melted |
| ⅓ cup milk | ½ teaspoon vanilla |
| ⅓ cup sugar | 2 tablespoons blueberries |
| 1 egg | 2 tablespoons white chocolate chips |

1. In a medium bowl, mix together the flour, milk, sugar, egg, butter, and vanilla *just* until smooth.

2. Fold the blueberries and white chocolate chips into the batter.

3. Divide the batter between 2 mugs, being careful not to fill the mugs more than half full.

4. Microwave each cake for about 1½ minutes, or until the top is firm but springy when lightly touched, and serve.

   *Topping Suggestion:* Streusel topping (page 164) is delicious on this cake—just spoon 1 to 2 tablespoons on top of the batter before baking. You can also use a Vanilla Glaze (page 171) for a mouthwatering finish.

   *Variation:* Use chopped maraschino cherries in place of the blueberries for a sweet cherry flavor.

# CHERRY-CHOCOLATE CHIP
## MUG CAKE

*Serves: 2  **Prep time:** 2 minutes  **Cook time:** 2 minutes*

This is sweet perfection for your favorite sweetheart. Although this cake is great anytime, it's just right for Valentine's Day dessert. Sweethearts young and old will love it. Add a spoonful of vanilla bean ice cream and drizzle hot fudge sauce over the top—it's gorgeous!

½ cup self-rising flour

⅓ cup milk

¼ cup sugar

1 egg

¼ cup unsalted butter, melted

2 tablespoons maraschino cherry juice

¼ cup mini chocolate chips

1. In a medium bowl, mix together the flour, milk, sugar, egg, butter, and cherry juice *just* until smooth.

2. Fold the chocolate chips into the batter.

3. Divide the batter between 2 mugs, being careful not to fill the mugs more than half full.

4. Microwave each mug for about 1 minute, or until the top is firm but springy when lightly touched, and serve.

*Topping Suggestion:* Use a shiny Chocolate Ganache (page 162) for a decadent finish to this cake.

*Make It Gluten-Free:* Use your preferred gluten-free flour to make this cake gluten-free. Add ⅛ teaspoon baking powder when switching from self-rising to any other flour. Check to make sure the chocolate chips are gluten-free, too.

*Variation:* Use white chocolate chips in place of the mini chocolate chips to give the cake a different flavor and texture.

# BANANA

*Serves: 2* **Prep time:** *2 minutes* **Cook time:** *2 minutes*

This moist banana cake comes together fast to make a fantastic bite to go with your afternoon coffee or afterschool snack. Make it in the morning while you're waiting for the coffee to brew and send it in a school lunch. Or, if you prefer, just call it a banana muffin and eat it for breakfast. We'll never tell.

| | |
|---|---|
| 1 very ripe banana, mashed | ¼ cup unsalted butter, melted |
| 1 egg | ½ cup self-rising flour |
| 2 tablespoons brown sugar | 2 tablespoons chopped pecans (optional) |
| 2 tablespoons granulated sugar | |

1. In a medium bowl, mix together the banana, egg, brown sugar, granulated sugar, and butter until smooth.

2. Add the flour, and stir *just* until smooth.

3. Fold the pecans (if using) into the batter.

4. Divide the batter between 2 mugs, being careful not to fill the mugs more than half full.

5. Microwave each cake for about 1 minute, or until the top is firm but springy when lightly touched, and serve.

*Topping Suggestion:* Salted Caramel Sauce (page 165) or a Vanilla Glaze (page 171) work really well on this cake. Try Cream Cheese Frosting (page 158) for something extra special.

*Variation:* Fold two tablespoons of mini chocolate chips into the batter for a surprise chocolate twist.

# BANANA-CHOCOLATE-PEANUT BUTTER
MUG CAKE

*Serves: 2  Prep time: 2 minutes  Cook time: 2 minutes*

This is the kid-friendliest of kid-friendly cakes, moist with a delightful blend of peanut butter and banana and a little chocolate in every bite. Let the littlest ones mash the bananas for this mug cake—it helps them feel like an important part of the process. If the batter seems too thick, add an extra teaspoon or two of milk to the batter.

1 very ripe banana, mashed

1 egg

2 tablespoons milk

2 tablespoons brown sugar

2 tablespoons granulated sugar

2 tablespoons unsalted butter, melted

2 tablespoons peanut butter

½ cup self-rising flour

2 tablespoons mini chocolate chips

1. In a medium bowl, mix together the banana, egg, milk, brown sugar, granulated sugar, butter, and peanut butter.

2. Add the flour, and stir *just* until smooth.

3. Fold the chocolate chips into the batter.

4. Divide the batter between 2 mugs, being careful not to fill the mugs more than half full.

5. Microwave each cake for about 1 minute, or until the top is firm but springy when lightly touched, and serve.

*Topping Suggestion:* Peanut Butter Frosting (page 160) is delicious on this cake. Make your cake extra special by grating a little chocolate over the top.

*Variation:* If peanut allergies are a problem, substitute almond butter for the peanut butter.

# APPLESAUCE

MUG CAKE

*Serves: 2  Prep time: 2 minutes  Cook time: 5 minutes*

Moist, hearty applesauce cake eaten warm right from the mug is the epitome of comfort food. The applesauce gives the cake moistness and flavor with the added bonus of less fat in this recipe than in others. You can cut the fat even more by using an egg white in place of the whole egg and replacing the 2 tablespoons of butter with an equal amount of applesauce.

| | |
|---|---|
| 2 tablespoons unsalted butter, melted | 1 egg |
| ¼ cup brown sugar | ½ cup self-rising flour |
| 2 tablespoons milk | ½ teaspoon ground cinnamon |
| 3 tablespoons applesauce | Pinch kosher salt |

1. In a medium bowl, mix together the butter and sugar until smooth.

2. Add the milk, applesauce, and egg, and beat until well mixed.

3. Add the flour, cinnamon, and salt, and stir *just* until smooth.

4. Divide the batter between 2 mugs, being careful not to fill the mugs more than half full.

5. Microwave each cake for 1½ to 2½ minutes on high, or until the top is firm but springy when lightly touched, and serve.

*Topping Suggestion:* Cinnamon sugar is a simple way to finish off this moist cake.

*Variation:* Fold up to 3 tablespoons of raisins into the batter for texture, flavor, and a little added nutrition.

# KEY LIME

*Serves: 2  **Prep time:** 2 minutes  **Cook time:** 2 minutes*

Key limes are so named because they grow in the Florida Keys. These tiny, yellow limes are loved for their sharp, tart acidity that lends brightness to any dish. If you're not able to find fresh key limes, many stores carry key lime juice next to the lemon and regular lime juices. If key lime juice is not available, you can substitute regular lime juice in an equal measure. If you like, make it fun for the kids by adding a few drops of green food color to the batter.

½ cup self-rising flour

¼ cup milk

1 egg

⅓ cup sugar

2 tablespoons vegetable oil

3 tablespoons freshly squeezed key lime juice

Zest of 1 lime

1.  In a medium bowl, mix together the flour, milk, egg, sugar, oil, lime juice, and lime zest *just* until smooth.

2.  Divide the batter between 2 mugs, being careful not to fill the mugs more than half full.

3.  Microwave each cake for about 1 minute, or until the cake is firm but springy when lightly touched, and serve.

*Topping Suggestion:* Cream Cheese Frosting (page 158) is the topping of choice on this. Its creaminess is a great balance to the tartness of the key lime.

*Make It Vegan:* This cake can be made vegan by substituting rice or almond milk for the milk and leaving out the egg.

*Variation:* White chocolate chips are delicious in this cake. Just fold 2 tablespoons into the batter.

# WHITE CHOCOLATE-RASPBERRY

## MUG CAKE

*Serves: 2  **Prep time:** 2 minutes  **Cook time:** 1½ minutes*

White chocolate and raspberry is a classic combination. In this recipe, the organic coconut oil adds healthy fats, moisture, and a delicate coconut flavor. It's an addictive combination of sweet and tangy that will handle your dessert cravings anytime. If fresh raspberries are out of season you can use thawed, well drained, frozen raspberries instead.

½ cup self-rising flour

2 tablespoons white chocolate chips

1 egg yolk

3 tablespoons sugar

1 tablespoon organic coconut oil

2 tablespoons buttermilk

¼ teaspoon of vanilla or almond extract

½ cup fresh raspberries

1. In a small bowl, combine the flour and the white chocolate chips.

2. In a separate bowl, combine the egg yolk, sugar, oil, buttermilk, and flavoring, and mix well.

3. Add the dry ingredients to the wet ingredients, and mix well.

4. Gently mix in the fresh raspberries.

5. Pour the mixture into two mugs, and microwave each for 1½ to 2 minutes.

6. Cool, then top with a dollop of whipped cream and a few more raspberries.

   *Topping Suggestion:* This cake is delicious with whipped cream, but to make it a little fancier try adding a teaspoon or two of black raspberry liqueur to the whipped cream as you whip it. Top with a few slices almonds if you wish.

   *Make It Vegan:* Leave out the egg yolk and use almond or coconut milk instead of the buttermilk. Add an extra teaspoon of coconut oil. Do check the white chocolate chips you are using to ensure that they are vegan as well.

# 6

## *Seasonal Favorites*

Coconut Mug Cake 71

Maple-Nut Mug Cake 72

Cherry Limeade Mug Cake 73

Pink Lemonade Mug Cake 74

Caramel Apple Mug Cake 75

Pumpkin Mug Cake 76

Gingerbread Mug Cake 77

Clementine Mug Cake 78

Earl Grey and Lemon Mug Cake 79

# ENJOY THE FLAVORS OF EACH SEASON

It's hard to imagine autumn without pumpkin, isn't it? Certain flavors just seem to go hand in hand with a particular season. Sometimes it has to do with the ingredient being plentiful at that time of year, while other times it's more about tradition and memories. Pink lemonade is delicious anytime, but it seems more enjoyable on a hot summer afternoon than a chilly winter morning.

To really kick up your mug cake, try mixing flavors based on the season. Lemon and coconut is a classic combination for spring, but white chocolate and amaretto is delicious, too. You can also try combining flavors from the "all year" list with flavors from the seasonal lists. Try peanut butter and salted caramel, for example. Here are some favorite flavors and the seasons they are most associated with:

## SPRING

* Almond
* Amaretto
* Irish cream liqueur
* Champagne
* Coconut
* Cream cheese
* Green tea
* Lemon
* Marshmallow
* Pineapple
* Pistachio
* Vanilla
* White chocolate

## SUMMER

* Berries
* Lemonade
* Lemon-lime
* Limeade
* Piña colada
* Strawberry
* Toasted marshmallows / s'mores
* Watermelon

## FALL

* Apple
* Caramel
* Chocolate
* Maple
* Pumpkin
* Salted caramel
* Spice
* Walnuts, pecans, hickory nuts

## WINTER

* Cinnamon
* Cloves
* Cranberry
* Dried fruit
* Eggnog
* Gingerbread
* Mocha
* Nutmeg
* Orange
* Peppermint
* Rum
* Tangerine

## FLAVORS THAT WORK ALL YEAR

* Banana
* Cherry
* Chocolate
* Coffee
* Peanut butter
* Vanilla

# COCONUT

*Serves: 2  Prep time: 2 minutes  Cook time: 4 minutes*

Coconut cake is a popular dessert for the Easter table in the South. Although delicious year round, there is something about the flavor that lets you know spring has sprung.

¼ cup coconut oil

¼ cup plus 2 tablespoons sugar

¼ cup milk

½ teaspoon clear vanilla extract

3 drops coconut extract (optional)

1 egg white, beaten until frothy

½ cup self-rising flour

¼ cup shredded, sweetened coconut, plus extra for serving

1. In a large bowl, mix together the coconut oil, sugar, milk, vanilla, coconut extract (if using), and egg white.

2. Add the flour to the bowl, and mix *just* until smooth.

3. Fold ¼ cup of shredded, sweetened coconut into the batter.

4. Divide the batter between 2 mugs, being careful not to fill the mugs more than half full.

5. Microwave each cake for 1 to 2 minutes, or until the top is firm but springy when lightly touched. Sprinkle with the extra shredded coconut before serving.

*Topping Suggestion:* Spread Vanilla Frosting (page 157) on the cake before sprinkling it with the shredded coconut. For something a little tangier, spoon Lemon Curd (page 166) over the cake.

*Variation:* Turn this mug cake into Easter bunnies by carefully turning the cake out of the mug. Let it cool before covering it with vanilla frosting. Make the rabbit's ears from flattened marshmallows, and attach them with toothpicks. Use another marshmallow for the tail. Draw the eyes, nose, and whiskers with the gel icing you can buy in small tubes. It's a fun activity for the kids.

# MAPLE-NUT

*Serves: 2  Prep time: 2 minutes  Cook time: 4 minutes*

Maple, although considered by most to be a fall flavor, is a product of the first warm days of spring. Real maple syrup is time-consuming and labor-intensive, but the final product is a taste of heaven. It's fun to read about how it's made and then make this mug cake. It gives everyone a new appreciation for just how special maple syrup really is.

2 tablespoons butter, melted

2 tablespoons sugar

3 tablespoons maple syrup

1 egg

1 tablespoon milk

⅓ cup self-rising flour

¼ cup chopped walnuts

1. In a large measuring cup or medium bowl, mix together the butter, sugar, maple syrup, egg, and milk.

2. Add the flour, and stir *just* until smooth.

3. Fold the walnuts into the batter.

4. Divide the batter between 2 mugs, being careful not to fill the mugs more than half full.

5. Microwave each cake for 2 minutes, or until the cake is firm but springy when lightly touched, and serve.

*Topping Suggestion:* Serve this cake warm from the microwave with a scoop of vanilla ice cream and more maple syrup drizzled over the top.

*Variation:* If you can find real maple sugar, use it in place of the granulated sugar called for in this recipe to boost the maple flavor of the cake.

# CHERRY LIMEADE

*Serves: 2  **Prep time:** 2 minutes  **Cook time:** 4 minutes*

Sweet cherry and tart lime flavors come together in this pretty cake to create one of the iconic flavor combinations of summer. Fun to serve at summer pool parties and picnics, this cake is so easy that older children can make a batch while the adults are grilling burgers and stirring up potato salad. Everyone gets something to do.

| | |
|---|---|
| 2 tablespoons vegetable or peanut oil | 3 tablespoons limeade concentrate |
| ¼ cup sugar | 2 tablespoons maraschino cherry juice |
| 1 egg | ½ cup self-rising flour |

1.  In a large measuring cup or medium bowl, mix together the oil, sugar, egg, limeade concentrate, and cherry juice.

2.  Add the flour, and stir *just* until smooth.

3.  Divide the batter between 2 mugs, being careful not to fill the mugs more than half full.

4.  Microwave each cake for 2 minutes, or until the cake is firm but springy when lightly touched, and serve.

*Topping Suggestion:* Dust this cake with a little confectioners' sugar before serving.

*Make It Vegan:* This works very well as a vegan cake, too. Just leave out the egg or replace it with your preferred vegan egg substitute.

*Variation:* Fold 2 tablespoons chopped maraschino cherries into the batter before cooking to intensify the cherry flavor.

# PINK LEMONADE

*Serves: 2  Prep time: 2 minutes  Cook time: 4 minutes*

Pink lemonade is the stuff of muggy summer days when everything seems to move in slow motion. These tangy mug cakes have that flavor right along with a pretty pink color, making them perfect for special occasions like the Fourth of July or a summer tea. For a pretty presentation, split this recipe into 4 parts and cook the cakes in dainty (microwave-safe) teacups instead of coffee mugs. Or the kids can make and offer these cakes as a new take on the lemonade stand.

2 tablespoons vegetable or peanut oil

¼ cup sugar

1 egg white

¼ cup milk

⅓ cup self-rising flour

1 tablespoon unsweetened pink lemonade powdered drink mix

1.  In a large measuring cup or medium bowl, mix together the oil, sugar, egg white, and milk.

2.  Add the flour and drink mix, and stir *just* until smooth.

3.  Divide the batter between 2 mugs, being careful not to fill the mugs more than half full.

4.  Microwave each cake for 2 minutes, or until the cake is firm but springy when lightly touched, and serve.

*Topping Suggestion:* Spoon Lemon Glaze (page 169) over the warm cake. The glaze gives it a little sweetness while complementing the tangy lemonade flavor.

*Variation:* Fold 1 tablespoon freshly grated lemon zest into the batter for more lemony goodness.

# CARAMEL APPLE

## MUG CAKE

*Serves: 2  **Prep time:** 2 minutes  **Cook time:** 4 minutes*

The beginning of cooler weather means it's time for county fairs and apple picking. This caramel apple mug cake hits every high note. The warm caramel is gooey, and the apples are both sweet and tart at the same time. Make these in tall jelly jars with screw-on tops—they sell really well at school bake sales. Fix a plastic spoon to the jar with some strands of raffia for a country-cute look.

1 tablespoon unsalted butter, melted

¼ cup unsweetened applesauce

2 tablespoons milk

⅓ cup sugar

½ cup self-rising flour

1 teaspoon apple pie spice

2 tablespoons Salted Caramel Sauce (page 165), divided

4 tablespoons apple pie filling, divided

1. In a large measuring cup or medium bowl, mix together the butter, applesauce, milk, and sugar.

2. Add the flour and apple pie spice, and stir *just* until smooth.

3. Divide the caramel sauce between 2 mugs, then top each with 2 tablespoons apple pie filling.

4. Divide the batter between the 2 mugs, being careful not to fill the mugs more than half full.

5. Microwave each cake for 2 minutes, or until the cake is firm but springy when lightly touched, and serve.

*Topping Suggestion:* Top the warm cake with a dollop of vanilla ice cream; then drizzle either Salted Caramel Sauce (page 165) or Bourbon Caramel Syrup (page 163) over the top.

*Variation:* Peeled, ripe Bosc pears work really well in this cake, delivering a burst of added sweetness. Fold 2 to 3 tablespoons into the batter.

# PUMPKIN

MUG CAKE

*Serves: 2  Prep time: 2 minutes  Cook time: 4 minutes*

Pumpkin is a warm, comforting flavor that speaks of crackling fires, crimson leaves, and the first brisk winds of the season. It has a natural sweetness that kids love, and it's full of vitamin A. On that first chilly evening, put out the ingredients for this pumpkin mug cake, add a couple of bowls of add-ins like chopped nuts and white chocolate chips, and let each member of the family make their own version of pumpkin cake to munch on after an afternoon of raking leaves or a day of touch football.

| | |
|---|---|
| 2 tablespoons butter, melted | 1 tablespoon milk |
| ¼ cup sugar | ¼ cup pumpkin purée |
| 2 tablespoons brown sugar | ⅓ cup self-rising flour |
| 1 egg | ½ teaspoon pumpkin pie spice |

1.  In a large measuring cup or medium bowl, mix together the butter, sugar, brown sugar, egg, milk, and pumpkin purée.

2.  Add the flour and pumpkin pie spice, and stir *just* until smooth.

3.  Divide the batter between 2 mugs, being careful not to fill the mugs more than half full.

4.  Microwave each cake for 2 minutes, or until the cake is firm but springy when lightly touched, and serve.

*Topping Suggestion:* Cream Cheese Frosting (page 158) or Streusel (page 164) would be perfect for this fall favorite. If you use the streusel, add it to the top of the batter before you cook the cakes.

*Make It Vegan:* This cake can be made vegan by substituting oil for the butter, leaving out the egg, and using almond milk.

*Variation:* Fold 2 tablespoons of toasted, chopped pecans into the batter before cooking.

# GINGERBREAD

*Serves: 2  Prep time: 2 minutes  Cook time: 4 minutes*

Gingerbread spans two seasons; its warm flavor is a welcome treat for fall or winter. These cakes make wonderful holiday gifts, too. Cook them in jelly jars and let them cool before putting on the lids. Tie plaid bows around the tops and they're ready to give to guests at your holiday party, as teachers' gifts, or for whatever the occasion may be. Use a blustery cold day a few days before your holiday party or the kids' winter school break, and make this a family project. This cake is quick, easy, inexpensive . . . and most of all, fun!

| | |
|---|---|
| 2 tablespoons butter, melted | ½ cup self-rising flour |
| ¼ cup brown sugar | 1 teaspoon ground ginger |
| 1 egg | ½ teaspoon ground cinnamon |
| 2 tablespoons milk | Pinch baking soda |
| 1 tablespoon unsulfured molasses | |

1.  In a large measuring cup or medium bowl, mix together the butter, brown sugar, egg, milk, and molasses.

2.  Add the flour, ginger, cinnamon, and baking soda, and stir *just* until smooth.

3.  Divide the batter between 2 mugs, being careful not to fill the mugs more than half full.

4.  Microwave each cake for 2 minutes, or until the cake is firm but springy when lightly touched, and serve.

    *Topping Suggestion:* Gingerbread is just right without any topping at all. If you would like a little extra something, a dollop of lightly sweetened whipped cream is delicious.

    *Make It Gluten-Free:* This cake can be made gluten-free by substituting 2 tablespoons coconut meal and 3 tablespoons almond meal for the flour called for in this recipe. It makes the gingerbread a little denser, but it'll be just as delicious.

    *Variation:* Fold 2 tablespoons chopped candied ginger into the batter for more ginger flavor.

# CLEMENTINE

*Serves: 2  Prep time: 2 minutes  Cook time: 4 minutes*

Clementines are tiny, sweet, easy-to-peel tangerines that are quite seasonal. They show up in the grocery stores around the beginning of November—just in time for the holidays. This cake is packed with that bright tangerine flavor. Make it in the morning while your coffee is brewing, and send it in a school lunch. It will brighten up the dreariest winter day.

¼ cup butter, melted

⅓ cup sugar

1 egg

¼ cup freshly squeezed clementine juice

1 teaspoon clementine zest

⅓ cup flour

Pinch baking soda

1.  In a large measuring cup or medium bowl, mix together the butter, sugar, egg, and juice until smooth.

2.  Add the zest, flour, and baking soda, and mix *just* until smooth.

3.  Divide the batter between 2 mugs, being careful not to fill the mugs more than half full.

4.  Microwave each cake for 2 minutes, or until the cake is firm but springy when lightly touched, and serve.

    *Topping Suggestion:* A drizzle of Vanilla Glaze (page 171) really brings out the flavor of this tangy cake. If you have time, peel a clementine and dip the bottom half of each section in melted chocolate. Arrange 2 or 3 sections on the top of each cake.

    *Make It Vegan:* Substitute oil for the butter and leave out the egg.

    *Variation:* Try a sweet red grapefruit in this cake instead of the clementines for a fresh, tangy flavor.

78 • THE ABSOLUTE BEST MUG CAKES COOKBOOK

# EARL GREY AND LEMON
## MUG CAKE

*Serves: 2  Prep time: 2 minutes  Cook time: 2 minutes, 3 minutes resting*

Is there anyone who doesn't like a cup of Earl Grey tea on a chilly, rainy spring afternoon? This cake takes those soul-warming flavors and makes them into something incredibly decadent. The tealeaves are used to infuse the most flavor into the cake. You can just use loose-leaf tea or tear open a regular tea bag.

| | |
|---|---|
| 2 tablespoons unsalted butter, melted | ½ teaspoon vanilla extract |
| ½ teaspoon Earl Grey tea leaves | 1 tablespoon milk |
| 1 tablespoon lemon zest | 1 tablespoon lemon juice |
| ¼ cup sugar | ⅓ cup self rising flour |
| 1 egg | |

1. Combine the butter and tea in a microwave-safe bowl.

2. Cook for 30 seconds, or until the butter is completely melted.

3. Set aside to cool for about 3 minutes.

4. When the butter mixture has cooled, whisk in the sugar, vanilla extract, milk, and lemon juice.

5. Mix the flour and lemon zest together and add to the wet ingredients.

6. Divide the batter into two mugs.

7. Microwave for 1 to 1½ minutes, or until the batter is firm.

*Topping Suggestion:* Lemon Glaze (page 169) is the perfect finish to this tangy, bright cake.

*Make It Gluten-Free:* Substitute your favorite gluten-free flour and add ½ teaspoon of baking soda.

*Variation:* Use tangerine or orange zest and juice instead of the lemon called for in this recipe. It gives it a mellower flavor that is comforting and delicious.

# 7

## *Birthdays*

Confetti Mug Cake *83*

Chocolate Confetti Mug Cake *84*

Mocha Mug Cake *85*

Chocolate Chip Mug Cake *86*

Chocolate Fudge Mug Cake *87*

Rainbow Mug Cake *88*

Butterscotch Mug Cake *90*

White Wedding Cake in a Mug *91*

Pink Cherry Mug Cake *92*

Salted Caramel Mug Cake *93*

# THERE'S NO PARTY LIKE A MUG CAKE PARTY

Making mug cakes the center of activity for a birthday party is a unique way to serve cake and give your guests a new experience. Plus it allows you to relax and enjoy the party, too. It's lots of fun. Here's how:

* Have everyone bring their favorite microwave-safe mug (and have extras on hand just in case someone forgets), or supply the mugs as a party favor.

* If supplying the mugs, try to get mugs that match your party theme or colors. You'll need to plan ahead to do this, but imagine how much fun it will be for kids to make their own mug cakes in a superhero mug at a superhero-themed party, for example.

* You can find inexpensive mugs at the dollar store, garage sales, and thrift shops. Always check them ahead of time to ensure they are safe for the microwave. To check, place an empty mug in the microwave along with a second mug with one cup of water in it. Microwave on high for one minute. The empty mug should be cool, and the water in the other mug should be hot.

* Pick out five mug cake recipes, and print all of them out on a sheet of paper. Depending on the number of guests, you may need multiple copies. You can even go so far as to laminate the recipes—spills wipe right off. Supply the ingredients, and let your guests pick and make their own cakes.

* If the party is for very young children, put the dry ingredients together in small, sealable bags (remember each recipe in this book will make two cakes, so two bags per recipe) so that the guests just have to add the liquid ingredients. It should help make things less messy.

* Make frosting choices ahead of the party, or you can purchase a variety of frosting flavors.

* Have lots of sprinkles, colored sugar, gummy bears, and other edible decorations available so your guests can create their very own masterpieces.

* When everyone is done, give prizes for the most creative, the most chocolate, the most beautiful, the fanciest, etc., mug cake. Try to have some kind of prize for each guest, especially if your party is for younger children.

* An inexpensive plastic tablecloth that coordinates with your birthday party theme or color will make cleanup much easier—just roll the whole thing up and throw it away.

* Keep in mind that each recipe in this book does make two mug cakes. The recipes are relatively easy to split in half—except for the egg. A large egg has about 3 tablespoons of liquid, so 1½ tablespoons of beaten egg would be needed for a single mug cake.

# CONFETTI

## MUG CAKE

*Serves: 2  **Prep time:** 2 minutes  **Cook time:** 5 minutes*

Confetti cakes are vanilla cakes with colored sprinkles folded in. The sprinkles add a lot of color without a lot of flavor. When you cut into a Confetti mug cake, it sings out "party!" like nothing else. This recipe has a whole teaspoon of vanilla for two cakes to give it a deeper vanilla flavor. You can cut that in half if you'd like. Sprinkles come in all kinds of colors and color combinations, so if you like, match the "confetti" to your child's preferred color palette, or to the theme of the occasion or holiday. Be creative, but most of all—have fun.

| | |
|---|---|
| ¼ cup unsalted butter, melted | 1 teaspoon vanilla |
| ¼ cup plus 2 tablespoons sugar | ½ cup self-rising flour |
| 1 egg | Pinch salt |
| ¼ cup milk | ¼ cup colored sprinkles or jimmies |

1. In a medium bowl, mix together the butter and sugar until smooth.

2. Add the egg, milk, and vanilla, and beat until well mixed.

3. Add the flour and salt, and stir *just* until smooth.

4. Fold the sprinkles into the batter.

5. Divide the batter between 2 mugs, being careful not to fill the mugs more than half full.

6. Microwave each cake for 1½ to 2½ minutes, or until the top is firm but springy when lightly touched, and serve.

   *Topping Suggestion:* Vanilla Frosting (page 157) or Chocolate Frosting (page 159) are the classic toppings to this cake. Add a few extra sprinkles for color. Don't forget the candle. After all, it's a celebration!

   *Variation:* Fold 2 tablespoons finely chopped gumdrops into the batter in place of the sprinkles for a sweet, chewy surprise.

# CHOCOLATE CONFETTI

*Serves: 2  Prep time: 2 minutes  Cook time: 5 minutes*

This mug cake is just like the Vanilla Confetti cake but for those chocolate fans in your life. Rich, moist chocolate cake has bursts of color
throughout. A word of warning, though: If the sprinkles are too small,
they will get lost. If you can find the colored circle sprinkles rather
than the smaller jimmies, they'll work better because they make
larger spots of color in the cake.

| | |
|---|---|
| ¼ cup unsalted butter, melted | ½ cup self-rising flour |
| ½ cup sugar | ¼ cup cocoa |
| ¼ cup plus 2 tablespoons milk | Pinch salt |
| 1 egg | ¼ cup colored sprinkles or jimmies |

1. In a medium bowl, mix together the butter and sugar
   until smooth.

2. Add the milk and egg and beat until well mixed.

3. Add the flour, cocoa, and salt, and stir *just* until smooth.

4. Fold the sprinkles into the batter.

5. Divide the batter between 2 mugs, being careful not to fill the
   mugs more than half full.

6. Microwave each cake for 1½ to 2½ minutes, or until the top is firm
   but springy when lightly touched, and serve.

*Topping Suggestion:* Chocolate Frosting (page 159) with added
sprinkles and a candle on top will make this mug cake colorful
and fun. A spoonful of marshmallow cream is also delicious.

*Make It Dairy-Free:* For a dairy-free version of this cake, substitute coconut milk and coconut oil for the milk and butter.

*Variation:* Make a chocolate polka dot cake by substituting white
chocolate chips for the sprinkles.

# MOCHA

*Serves:* 2 *Prep time:* 2 *minutes* *Cook time:* 5 *minutes*

Mocha is that perfect balance between chocolate and coffee that creates a flavor all its own. Brew espresso or espresso-strength coffee to use in this mug cake. Another option is to add 1 teaspoon instant coffee granules along with the coffee to the cake batter to give it a more intense coffee flavor.

| | |
|---|---|
| ¼ cup unsalted butter, melted | ¼ cup self-rising flour |
| ¼ cup sugar | ¼ cup cocoa |
| 1 egg | Pinch salt |
| ¼ cup strong, cold espresso | |

1. In a medium bowl, mix together the butter and sugar until smooth.

2. Add the egg and espresso, and beat until well mixed.

3. Add the flour, cocoa, and salt, and stir *just* until smooth.

4. Fold the sprinkles into the batter.

5. Divide the batter between 2 mugs, being careful not to fill the mugs more than half full.

6. Microwave each cake for 1½ to 2½ minutes, or until the top is firm but springy when lightly touched, and serve.

*Topping Suggestion:* Creamy Chocolate Frosting (page 159) is so good on this cake that it's hard to stop with just one.

*Variation:* Fold 1 tablespoon cacao nibs into the batter to boost the chocolate flavor and give a little more texture to the finished cake.

# CHOCOLATE CHIP

## MUG CAKE

*Serves: 2  Prep time: 2 minutes  Cook time: 4 minutes*

Mmmmm. . . . A tall glass of milk and a chocolate chip mug cake. Nothing says welcome home better than that. This moist yellow cake has just a hint of brown sugar to give it that faint caramel flavor found in your favorite chocolate chip cookie. Add 2 tablespoons of chopped pecans if you want a little added crunch.

| | |
|---|---|
| ¼ cup unsalted butter, melted | ¼ cup milk |
| 3 tablespoons brown sugar | ½ cup self-rising flour |
| 3 tablespoons granulated sugar | Pinch salt |
| 1 egg | ¼ cup mini chocolate chips |

1. In a medium bowl, combine the butter, brown sugar, granulated sugar, egg, and milk. Mix until smooth.

2. Add the flour and salt, and stir *just* until smooth.

3. Fold the chocolate chips into the batter.

4. Divide the batter between 2 mugs, being careful not to fill the mugs more than half full.

5. Microwave each cake for 1 to 2 minutes, or until the top is firm but springy when lightly touched, and serve.

*Topping Suggestion:* Chocolate Frosting (page 159) is the perfect choice for this mug cake.

*Make It Gluten-Free:* Use your favorite gluten-free flour, or try substituting coconut flour for half the gluten-free flour. Whenever you substitute gluten-free flour, remember to add ⅛ teaspoon of baking powder unless you are using your own homemade, self-rising gluten-free flour.

*Variation:* Substitute white chocolate chips for the chocolate chips, and fold 2 tablespoons chopped macadamia nuts into the batter.

# CHOCOLATE FUDGE

*Serves: 2* **Prep time:** *2 minutes* **Cook time:** *4 minutes*

Hosting an unexpected play date? Put a variety of add-ins in muffin tins (chocolate chips, nuts, chopped candy bars, etc.), and let kids create their own chocolate masterpieces. The brown sugar in this recipe makes it extra moist and fudgy, but you can add a few tablespoons of your favorite candy bar chopped up if you'd like to. You know, just because. Err on the side of undercooking this a little to keep it deliciously gooey.

¼ cup unsalted butter, melted

¼ cup brown sugar

¼ cup milk

1 egg

½ teaspoon vanilla

¼ cup self-rising flour

¼ cup cocoa powder

1. In a medium bowl, mix the butter, brown sugar, milk, egg, and vanilla until smooth.

2. Add the flour and cocoa, and stir *just* until smooth.

3. Divide the batter between 2 mugs, being careful not to fill the mugs more than half full.

4. Microwave each cake for 1 to 2 minutes, or until the top is firm but springy when lightly touched, and serve.

   *Topping Suggestion:* Chocolate Frosting (page 159) or Praline Glaze (page 170) are perfect choices for this mug cake.

   *Make It Sugar-Free:* Substitute any sugar-free sweetener in equal measure to the brown sugar.

   *Variation:* Brown the butter in a small saucepan on the stove by letting it melt; continue to cook (watching it carefully) until it is a golden brown color. Use this in place of the melted butter in this recipe to give the cake a nutty, rich taste.

# RAINBOW

*Serves: 2  Prep time: 2 minutes  Cook time: 5 minutes*

This cake batter needs to be white, otherwise your colors will be off when you stir in the food coloring. Using oil, egg white, and clear vanilla ensures that you'll get a full blast of rainbow color. Gel or paste colors will give you more color intensity than liquid food color, but add it a little at a time. Be careful with red—it will give your cake a bitter flavor if you use too much. This cake is a blast, letting kids create their own rainbow designs.

¼ cup vegetable or peanut oil

¼ cup sugar

¼ cup milk

1 egg white, beaten until foamy

½ teaspoon clear vanilla extract

½ cup self-rising flour

Pinch salt

3 liquid food colors, such as red, blue, and yellow

1. In a medium bowl or large measuring cup, mix together the oil, sugar, milk, egg white, and vanilla until smooth.

2. Add the flour and salt, stirring *just* until blended.

3. Divide the batter between 3 small bowls and add a few drops of food coloring to each bowl to get the colors you want.

4. Add alternating spoonfuls of the colored batter to 2 mugs, being careful not to fill the mugs more than half full. Then pull a clean knife through the batter in the mugs to make swirls.

5. Microwave each cake for 1½ to 2½ minutes, or until the top is firm but springy when lightly touched, and serve.

*Topping Suggestion:* Vanilla Frosting (page 157) is pretty on this cake and helps show off the cake colors. Garnish with some rainbow sprinkles, too.

*Make It Sugar-Free:* You can use a measure-for-measure sugar substitute to make this a sugar-free cake. Instead of vanilla frosting, top it with a little sugar-free vanilla yogurt. Some people don't like to use artificial coloring. If you prefer, you can use the natural food colorings available at some natural food stores.

*Variation:* Add ½ teaspoon unsweetened powdered drink mix in different flavors to the different colors—blue raspberry for blue, strawberry for pink, etc., for added flavor bursts.

# BUTTERSCOTCH

*Serves: 2 Prep time: 2 minutes Cook time: 4 minutes*

One bite of this rich cake, and you'll be overcome by that old-fashioned butterscotch flavor. Brown sugar, vanilla, and extra butter flavor kick this incredible dessert up a notch. Replace a tablespoon of the milk with a tablespoon of scotch or bourbon for an even deeper flavor and a grown-up cake. Hey, some days just require it!

| | |
|---|---|
| ¼ cup unsalted butter, melted | ¼ teaspoon vanilla |
| ¼ cup brown sugar | ¼ teaspoon butter flavoring |
| 1 egg | ½ cup self-rising flour |
| ¼ cup milk | Pinch salt |

1.  In a medium bowl, mix together the butter and brown sugar until smooth.

2.  Add the egg, milk, vanilla, and butter flavoring, and beat until well mixed.

3.  Add the flour and salt, stirring *just* until smooth.

4.  Divide the batter between 2 mugs, being careful not to fill the mugs more than half full.

5.  Microwave each cake for 1 to 2 minutes, or until the top is firm but springy when lightly touched, and serve.

    *Topping Suggestion:* Salted Caramel Sauce (page 165), Vanilla Frosting (page 157), or Rum Glaze (page 168) are all great toppings for this cake.

    *Variation:* Make a golden sundae by using this cake as a base for Butter Brickle ice cream—then drizzle it with warm butterscotch sauce. Top with whipped cream and a sprinkle of chopped pecans.

# WHITE WEDDING CAKE

IN A MUG

*Serves: 2  Prep time: 2 minutes  Cook time: 4 minutes*

This pretty, pure white cake has the same faint almond flavor that you find in wedding cakes, but the coconut oil gives it just a hint of coconut, too. It's light, delicate, and just right for a very special birthday or celebration. It's a great dessert for a bridal shower served in mugs that match the wedding colors!

¼ cup coconut oil

¼ cup plus 2 tablespoons sugar

¼ cup milk

½ teaspoon clear vanilla extract

3 drops almond extract

1 egg white, beaten until frothy

½ cup self-rising flour

1. In a medium bowl, mix together the coconut oil, sugar, milk, vanilla, almond extract, and egg white until completely incorporated.

2. Add the flour, and mix *just* until smooth.

3. Divide the batter between 2 mugs, being careful not to fill the mugs more than half full.

4. Microwave each cake for 1 to 2 minutes on high, or until the top is firm but springy when lightly touched, and serve.

*Topping Suggestion:* Vanilla Frosting (page 157) or Cream Cheese Frosting (page 158) flavored with a drop or two of almond extract will bring out the entire spectrum of flavor in this delicious cake.

*Make It Vegan:* You can make this cake vegan by substituting coconut milk for the milk and leaving out the egg.

*Variation:* Fold 2 tablespoons white chocolate chips into the batter before cooking for an even more decadent cake.

# PINK CHERRY

*Serves: 2  **Prep time:** 2 minutes  **Cook time:** 4 minutes*

A delicate pink cake is perfect for a birthday. Create magic by swirling a white frosting over the top and dusting it with edible white glitter or big sugar crystals. The flavor is sweet and light cherry vanilla, and the maraschino cherry juice gives this pretty mug cake its color.

¼ cup coconut oil, cold

¼ cup sugar

3 tablespoons milk

1 tablespoon maraschino cherry juice

1 egg white, beaten until frothy

¼ teaspoon clear vanilla extract

½ cup self-rising flour

1. In a medium bowl, mix together the oil, sugar, milk, cherry juice, egg white, and vanilla until smooth.

2. Add the flour, stirring *just* until smooth.

3. Divide the batter between 2 mugs, being careful not to fill the mugs more than half full.

4. Microwave each cake for 1 to 2 minutes, or until the top is firm but springy when lightly touched, and serve.

*Topping Suggestion:* Cream Cheese Frosting (page 158) is a delicious topping for this cake, but warm Chocolate Ganache (page 162) spooned over the top is really good, too.

*Variation:* Chopped toasted almonds work really well here. Fold 2 tablespoons into the batter before cooking.

# SALTED CARAMEL

*Serves: 2  Prep time: 2 minutes  Cook time: 3 minutes*

There is something addictive about that salty and sweet combination, whether it's chocolate-covered pretzels or salted caramel. Fleur de sel is a flaked, delicate sea salt available in most grocery stores. If you can't find it, use a few sea salt crystals sparingly. The caramels make the topping for this cake, so it needs no other garnish.

¼ cup unsalted butter, melted

¼ cup sugar

2 tablespoons brown sugar

¼ cup milk

½ teaspoon vanilla extract

1 egg

2 tablespoons Salted Caramel Sauce (page 165)

½ cup self-rising flour

1 teaspoon fleur de sel salt or other flaked sea salt, divided

2 caramel candies

1.  In a medium bowl, mix together the butter, sugar, brown sugar, milk, vanilla, egg, and Salted Caramel Sauce until smooth.

2.  Add the flour and ½ teaspoon of fleur de sel, mixing *just* until smooth.

3.  Divide the batter between 2 mugs, being careful not to fill the mugs more than half full.

4.  Microwave each cake for 30 seconds.

5.  Add one caramel to the top of each cake, and sprinkle each cake with the remaining fleur de sel.

6.  Microwave each cake for 1 more minute, or until firm, and serve.

*Topping Suggestion:* These don't need a topping at all—the caramel candies do that. If you want something extra on it, then a drizzle of Salted Caramel Sauce (page 165) will do the trick.

*Variation:* Fold 3 tablespoons chopped pretzels or chopped, salted peanuts into the batter before cooking.

# 8

## *Holidays*

Hot Chocolate and Marshmallow Mug Cake *97*

White Chocolate–Peppermint Mug Cake *98*

Vanilla Chai Mug Cake *99*

Eggnog Mug Cake *100*

Pumpkin Spice and Chipotle Mug Cake *101*

Red Velvet Mug Cake *102*

Chocolate-Covered Cherry Mug Cake *103*

Pineapple-Coconut Mug Cake *104*

Red, White, and Blue Mug Cake *105*

Hummingbird Mug Cake *106*

Irish Cream Mug Cake *107*

# GIVE THE GIFT OF A MUG CAKE

Holiday celebrations are the perfect time to express your appreciation to those who mean the most to you, and nothing shows that appreciation more than a thoughtful gift you made yourself. A gift of a mug cake might be exactly what you're looking for, great to present to a party host or hostess as a thank-you or as an activity for young and old(er) at your own holiday gathering. No matter how you employ the mug cake, it's sure to be a holiday hit.

To make the mug cake a gift:

* Find appropriate holiday-themed microwave-safe mugs at an affordable price at the dollar store.
* Mix the dry ingredients in a small, sealable plastic bag—snack size is best. Put any extras like chocolate chips in separate bags. Put the bags in the mug.
* Print the instructions on nice paper, and make a tag to tie onto the mug handle.
* Wrap the mug in cellophane tied off with a pretty ribbon, or place it in a gift bag.

Here are some ideas for themed baskets with the mug cake as the star and other treats to celebrate the holiday or other significant events.

* Make a chocolate-themed basket with a mocha mug cake, a chocolate-themed mug, some hot chocolate mixes, candies, and other chocolate-themed items. Perfect for Valentine's Day.
* A *When Life Gives You Lemons* basket can include a lemon mug cake mix, a mug sporting pictures of lemons, some lemonade mix, lemon drops candy, and a lemon-scented candle. Great for a summer-beginning or summer-ending Memorial Day or Labor Day barbecue.
* There's nothing like a snowy day basket with hot chocolate mix, a White Chocolate–Peppermint Mug Cake mix (page 98), and a favorite Christmas movie.
* Create a brunch basket for two with Blueberry Crumb Mug Cake mixes, using dried blueberries in place of fresh (page 112), coffee, tea, hot chocolate, and fresh fruit. It's a lovely way to celebrate a bridal or baby shower.
* Choose a book by a favorite author, and create a themed basket around that. Creativity abounds with this one.

There are as many possibilities for mug cake gifts as there are people on your list. Once you've decided on a theme, the rest is easy. Just remember that each recipe in this book makes two cakes, so you'll need to either cut the ingredients in half or add two mugs to the basket.

# HOT CHOCOLATE AND MARSHMALLOW
### · M U G  C A K E ·

*Serves: 2  **Prep time:** 2 minutes  **Cook time:** 5 minutes*

Warm, gooey chocolate cake with a melty, sticky marshmallow topping is hard to beat. What could be more rich and comforting than hot chocolate in cake form? Make sure you slightly undercook this mug cake and serve it hot to get the best texture. This may be quick and easy, but it's not less special—especially on the eve of a winter holiday.

| | |
|---|---|
| ¼ cup unsalted butter | ½ teaspoon vanilla extract |
| 1 ounce milk chocolate | ¼ cup self-rising flour |
| ¼ cup sugar | ¼ cup cocoa |
| ¼ cup milk | ¼ cup mini marshmallows, divided |
| 1 egg | |

1. In a medium, microwave-safe bowl, microwave the butter and milk chocolate for 1 minute. Stir together until smooth.

2. Add the sugar, milk, egg, vanilla, flour, and cocoa, and stir *just* until smooth.

3. Divide the batter between 2 mugs, being careful not to fill the mugs more than half full, and add ⅛ cup mini marshmallows to each mug.

4. Microwave each cake for 1 to 2 minutes, or until firm but still slightly gooey and the marshmallows are melted, and serve.

*Topping Suggestion:* Whipped cream and grated chocolate work well on this cake if you want something besides the marshmallows.

*Make It Gluten-Free:* Substitute gluten-free flour for the flour and adding ⅛ teaspoon baking powder.

*Variation:* Folding 2 tablespoons bittersweet chocolate chips into the batter will add depth to the chocolate flavor.

# WHITE CHOCOLATE-PEPPERMINT
## MUG CAKE

*Serves: 2  Prep time: 2 minutes  Cook time: 4 minutes*

Dreamy, rich white chocolate and crunchy, cool peppermint team up in this cake for a flavor that is filled with wintery magic. This mug cake makes an attractive gift if you layer the sugar, flour, white chocolate, and peppermint candy in a jelly jar with a screw-top lid. Tie a tag onto the jar with instructions for making the cake, then put it in a basket with two winter-themed mugs.

¼ cup vegetable or peanut oil

¼ cup plus 2 tablespoons sugar

¼ cup milk

½ teaspoon clear vanilla extract

3 drops almond extract

1 egg white, beaten until frothy

½ cup self-rising flour

¼ cup chopped white chocolate

¼ cup crushed peppermint candy

1. In a medium bowl, mix together the oil, sugar, milk, vanilla, almond extract, and egg white until smooth.

2. Add the flour, white chocolate, and peppermint candy, and mix *just* until smooth.

3. Divide the batter between 2 mugs, being careful not to fill the mugs more than half full.

4. Microwave each cake for 1 to 2 minutes, or until the top is firm but springy when lightly touched, and serve.

*Topping Suggestion:* Vanilla Glaze (page 171) is just right on this rich cake, but for a fancier presentation, use Vanilla Frosting (page 157) with crushed peppermint candy sprinkled on top.

*Variation:* Substitute ½ cup chopped white chocolate peppermint bark for the white chocolate and peppermint in this recipe.

# VANILLA CHAI
## MUG CAKE

*Serves: 2* **Prep time:** *4 minutes* **Cook time:** *2 minutes*

Chai is a tea spiced with cardamom, black pepper, cinnamon, and other spices. It is very comforting on a cold afternoon. This cake takes those flavors and brings them into cake form. Moist, spicy, and fragrant—this is the cake you want as you curl up by the fire with a book. It's also great for a late-night, post-Thanksgiving dinner second (or fourth) dessert.

¼ cup milk

2 tea bags, chai flavor

2 tablespoons vegetable oil

¼ cup sugar

½ teaspoon pure vanilla extract

1 egg

½ cup self-rising flour

1. In a microwave-safe mug, microwave the milk for 1 minute, or until bubbly. Add the tea bags to the milk and allow them to steep for 3 minutes.

2. Remove the tea bags from the milk, squeezing out the excess liquid before discarding the bags.

3. In a medium bowl, stir together the tea-infused milk, oil, sugar, vanilla, and egg until smooth.

4. Add the flour, and stir *just* until smooth.

5. Divide the batter between 2 mugs, being careful not to fill the mugs more than half full.

6. Microwave each cake for 1 minute, or until firm but springy when lightly touched, and serve.

*Topping Suggestion:* Vanilla Glaze (page 171) or Rum Glaze (page 168) are a perfect complement to the vanilla chai cake.

*Make It Dairy-Free:* Need a dairy-free version of this cake? Increase the oil to 3 tablespoons and replace the milk with water.

*Variation:* Any tea can be used in place of the chai. Try adding 2 Earl Grey tea bags and 1 tablespoon orange zest to the hot milk.

# EGGNOG

*Serves: 2  Prep time: 2 minutes  Cook time: 4 minutes*

Eggnog is a favorite Christmas drink. Intensely sweet, rich, and spiked (for the grown-ups) with a little rum—it's the stuff holiday dreams are made of. This is a fun family project to do right before trimming the tree. Or leave one for Santa instead of cookies—and maybe a Carrot Cake in a Mug (page 40) for the reindeer. Freshly grated nutmeg adds extra depth to this mug cake.

2 tablespoons vegetable or peanut oil

½ cup sugar

⅓ cup eggnog

½ teaspoon vanilla

1 tablespoon rum or ¼ teaspoon rum flavoring

1 egg

½ cup self-rising flour

Small pinch freshly grated nutmeg

1.  In a large measuring cup or medium bowl, combine the oil, sugar, eggnog, vanilla, rum, and egg. Mix together until smooth.

2.  Add the flour and nutmeg, and stir *just* until smooth.

3.  Divide the batter between 2 mugs, being careful not to fill the mugs more than half full.

4.  Microwave each cake for 2 minutes, or until the cake is firm but springy when lightly touched, and serve.

*Topping Suggestion:* Rum Glaze (page 168) and an extra sprinkle of nutmeg are the only toppings you'll need to finish off this cake.

*Variation:* Fold 2 tablespoons finely chopped walnuts into the batter before cooking for a satisfying crunch.

# PUMPKIN SPICE AND CHIPOTLE

## MUG CAKE

*Serves: 2  **Prep time:** 2 minutes  **Cook time:** 4 minutes*

The first chilly days of autumn generally bring out the craving for pumpkin recipes. This cake is moist and spicy, and every bite is full of mellow pumpkin flavor with just a kick of spicy pepper. Just be sure you're using pumpkin purée and not pumpkin pie filling. Top each cake with orange frosting, then flatten and cut black gumdrops to make a fun, jack-o'-lantern face. What a great Halloween party surprise!

| | |
|---|---|
| 2 tablespoons butter, melted | 2 tablespoons pumpkin purée |
| ¼ cup sugar | ⅓ cup self-rising flour |
| 1 egg | ½ teaspoon pumpkin pie spice |
| 3 tablespoons milk | Pinch powdered chipotle or cayenne pepper |

1.  In a large measuring cup or medium bowl, mix the butter, sugar, egg, milk, and pumpkin purée until smooth.

2.  Add the flour, pumpkin pie spice, and chipotle pepper, and stir *just* until smooth.

3.  Divide the batter between 2 mugs, being careful not to fill the mugs more than half full.

4.  Microwave each cake for 2 minutes, or until the cake is firm but springy when lightly touched, and serve.

*Topping Suggestion:* Cream Cheese Frosting (page 158) or Salted Caramel Sauce (page 165) both finish this cake with Halloween style. A scoop of vanilla ice cream never hurts either.

*Make It Vegan:* For a vegan version of this cake, substitute oil for the butter, leave out the egg, and use almond milk.

*Variation:* Use mashed sweet potato or acorn squash in place of the pumpkin purée.

# RED VELVET

*Serves: 2  Prep time: 2 minutes  Cook time: 4 minutes*

Red velvet cake is an iconic holiday dessert with a poinsettia-red color. It gets its flavor from just a touch of cocoa and a bit of red food coloring. You can adjust the amount of coloring up or down to get the exact color you want. If you're a culinary rebel, you can make this cake blue, green, or any other deep color by changing the food coloring you use.

| | |
|---|---|
| ¼ cup vegetable or peanut oil | 1 teaspoon liquid red food coloring |
| ⅓ cup sugar | ½ teaspoon vanilla extract |
| 1 egg | ⅓ cup plus 1 tablespoon self-rising flour |
| 3 tablespoons milk | 1 tablespoon cocoa |

1. In a large measuring cup or medium bowl, mix the oil, sugar, egg, milk, food coloring, and vanilla until smooth.

2. Add the flour and cocoa, and stir *just* until smooth.

3. Divide the batter between 2 mugs, being careful not to fill the mugs more than half full.

4. Microwave each cake for 2 minutes, or until the cake is firm but springy when lightly touched, and serve.

   *Topping Suggestion:* Add a generous spoonful of fluffy Cream Cheese Frosting (page 158) when serving this beautiful cake.

   *Variation:* Fold 2 tablespoons white chocolate chips into the batter. It's pretty and delicious.

# CHOCOLATE-COVERED CHERRY
## MUG CAKE

*Serves: 2  **Prep time:** 2 minutes  **Cook time:** 4 minutes*

Moist, dark chocolate cake with bits of cherry and chocolate chips generously mixed in is a perfect quick dessert for a romantic Valentine's Day dinner. If you eat it while it's still warm, the chocolate chips will be perfectly gooey. Make it pretty by decorating the plate with drizzled warm Chocolate Ganache (page 162) and placing the cake on top of the drizzle.

¼ cup butter, melted

⅓ cup sugar

1 egg

2 tablespoons milk

2 tablespoons maraschino cherry juice

⅓ cup self-rising flour

¼ cup cocoa

3 tablespoons chopped maraschino cherries

3 tablespoons mini chocolate chips

1. In a large measuring cup or medium bowl, mix the butter, sugar, egg, milk, and cherry juice until smooth.

2. Add the flour and cocoa, and stir *just* until smooth.

3. Fold the chopped cherries and chocolate chips into the batter.

4. Divide the batter between 2 mugs, being careful not to fill the mugs more than half full.

5. Microwave each cake for 2 minutes, or until the cake is firm but springy when lightly touched, and serve.

*Topping Suggestion:* Drizzle this spectacular cake with warm Chocolate Ganache (page 162), add a dollop of whipped cream, and top with a cherry.

*Make It Gluten-Free:* Substitute your favorite gluten-free flour for the self-rising flour.

*Variation:* Push a real chocolate-covered cherry into the center of the batter before cooking for a delicious surprise.

# PINEAPPLE-COCONUT
## MUG CAKE

*Serves: 2  Prep time: 2 minutes  Cook time: 4 minutes*

Somewhere between ambrosia and a piña colada, this Pineapple-Coconut Mug Cake is a two-minute vacation. It smells wonderful, and it's moist and full of the tropical flavors that sweep you away to the Caribbean—even when it's snowing outside. Slip a family-friendly beach movie into the DVD player and enjoy these cakes for family night.

3 tablespoons coconut oil

¼ cup sugar

1 egg

2 tablespoons piña colada mix

2 tablespoons pineapple juice

½ cup self-rising flour

2 tablespoons toasted coconut flakes

1. In a large measuring cup or medium bowl, combine the oil, sugar, egg, piña colada mix, and pineapple juice. Mix together until smooth.

2. Add the flour and toasted coconut, and stir *just* until smooth.

3. Divide the batter between 2 mugs, being careful not to fill the mugs more than half full.

4. Microwave each cake for 2 minutes, or until the cake is firm but springy when lightly touched, and serve.

*Cooking Tip:* To toast the coconut flakes, preheat the oven to 350°F. Spread the coconut flakes in a thin layer on a baking sheet and bake for about 20 minutes, until lightly browned, stirring occasionally.

*Topping Suggestion:* Top this cake with Rum Glaze (page 168) and sprinkle with a little extra toasted coconut.

*Variation:* Make these a day ahead of time and soak them in some rum. Grease the mugs before adding the batter to them so the cakes can be easily removed. Adults only, please.

# RED, WHITE, AND BLUE
## MUG CAKE

*Serves: 2  Prep time: 2 minutes  Cook time: 4 minutes*

Wave the flag for this perfect summer dessert. The cake is sweet and light with tangy berries in each bite. You can easily substitute raspberries or cherries for the strawberries in this recipe if you like. Do make sure the berries are well drained, or the cake will be soggy. Light up the Fourth of July by putting a candle or a lit sparkler in the top of the cakes when you serve them.

| | |
|---|---|
| 3 tablespoons vegetable or peanut oil | ½ teaspoon clear vanilla extract |
| ½ cup sugar | ½ cup self-rising flour |
| 1 egg white | ¼ cup fresh blueberries |
| ¼ cup milk | ¼ cup chopped strawberries, drained |

1. In a large measuring cup or medium bowl, mix together the oil, sugar, egg white, milk, and vanilla until smooth.

2. Add the flour, and stir *just* until smooth.

3. Fold the blueberries and strawberries into the batter.

4. Divide the batter between 2 mugs, being careful not to fill the mugs more than half full.

5. Microwave each cake for 2 minutes, or until the cake is firm but springy when lightly touched, and serve.

*Topping Suggestion:* Top with Cream Cheese Frosting (page 158) or just a simple dollop of whipped cream.

*Make It Sugar-Free:* Use your favorite measure-for-measure sugar-free sweetener. Top with some fresh fruit or whipped cream lightly sweetened with the same sweetener.

*Variation:* Add 1 tablespoon finely grated orange zest and ½ teaspoon orange extract for the vanilla in this recipe. Lemon zest and extract works beautifully, too.

# HUMMINGBIRD
MUG CAKE

*Serves: 2  Prep time: 2 minutes  Cook time: 2 minutes*

Hummingbird cake is a Southern tradition for the winter holidays. It is dense and sweet with a lot of fruit flavor from the banana and pineapple. The almond flour gives the cake some extra texture and holds up well to the fruit. Pecans are the traditional nut used in this cake, giving additional texture and crunch to every bite.

¼ cup very ripe banana, mashed

1 tablespoon pineapple juice

1 egg

2 tablespoons brown sugar

2 tablespoons granulated sugar

¼ cup unsalted butter, melted

¼ cup self-rising flour

¼ cup almond flour

2 tablespoons crushed pineapple, drained well

2 tablespoons chopped pecans (optional)

1. In a medium bowl, mix together the banana, pineapple juice, egg, brown sugar, granulated sugar, and melted butter. Mix until smooth.

2. Add the self-rising flour and almond flour, and stir *just* until smooth.

3. Fold the crushed pineapple and chopped pecans (if using) into the batter.

4. Divide the batter between 2 mugs, being careful not to fill the mugs more than half full.

5. Microwave each cake for about 1 minute, or until the top is firm but springy when lightly touched, and serve.

*Topping Suggestion:* Cream Cheese Frosting (page 158) all the way on this sweet cake. There's no better topping than that.

*Variation:* While pecans are traditional, you can use walnuts, almonds, macadamias, or any nut you prefer.

# IRISH CREAM
## MUG CAKE

*Serves: 2  **Prep time:** 2 minutes  **Cook time:** 2 minutes*

Irish cream is a favorite flavor all year, but it has a special place at the St. Patrick's Day table. This grown-up mug cake is a quick treat with a creamy, boozy flavor perfect for marking the coming of spring. Serve it with a mug of Irish coffee and drizzle warm ganache on top of the cake for a sweet and potent dessert.

¼ cup butter, melted

½ cup sugar

1 egg

2 tablespoons milk

2 tablespoons Irish cream liqueur

½ cup self-rising flour

1. In a large measuring cup or medium bowl, mix together the butter, sugar, egg, milk, and liquor until smooth.

2. Add the flour, and stir *just* until smooth.

3. Divide the batter between 2 mugs, being careful not to fill the mugs more than half full.

4. Microwave each cake for 2 minutes, or until the cake is firm but springy when lightly touched, and serve.

*Topping Suggestion:* A simple Vanilla Glaze (page 171) works well on this cake.

*Make It Gluten-Free:* Substitute any gluten-free flour in this recipe. Just remember to add ⅛ teaspoon baking powder.

*Variation:* Make this cake nonalcoholic and kid friendly by using ¼ cup Irish cream coffee creamer in place of the milk and liqueur.

# 9

## *Cake for Breakfast*

Cinnamon Roll Mug Cake *111*

Blueberry Crumb Mug Cake *112*

Banana-Nut Mug Cake *113*

Doughnut in a Mug *114*

Maple-Bacon Mug Cake *115*

Raspberry–Coffee Cake in a Mug *116*

Oatmeal-Raisin Mug Cake *117*

Crumb Cake in a Mug *118*

Easy Pancakes and Bacon Mug Cake *119*

# HAVE A WEEKEND MUG CAKE BREAKFAST

Mug cakes for breakfast? Why not? Whether hosting guests for the weekend or just having your family go in 10 different directions, mug cakes can provide a satisfying breakfast to start your day. From blueberry muffins to crumb cake, you can make almost any kind of breakfast bread quickly and easily in a mug right in your microwave. That's going to be way better than (not to mention just as quick as) cereal before a soccer game, right?

Rather than making a big production out of breakfast for house guests, let them make their favorite muffins. In just a few minutes, a piping hot, fresh breakfast will be ready. Pre-measure the dry ingredients and provide the recipe instructions, and everyone can custom make their own breakfast in their own time. Since each recipe in this book makes two servings, if the second one isn't wanted right away, it can be saved for later or frozen.

Kids can create a special Mother's Day or Father's Day breakfast in bed with a breakfast mug cake. Continue the fun of last night's slumber party with a self-serve brunch bar. Or make a variety of mug cakes, plate them on serving dishes, and slice them. Serve with small bowls of butter, honey, cream cheese, jelly, jam, and fresh fruit. Put a thermal carafe full of coffee nearby with cream and sugar and a pitcher or two of juice, and you have the easiest brunch ever.

A mug cake breakfast basket with mug cake mix, a couple of mugs, and a few other breakfast goodies is a really nice "Welcome to the Neighborhood" gift, too.

Mug cakes are easy to make, and they give even the least-experienced cook a chance to make something special without much fuss and still have time to enjoy the party.

# CINNAMON ROLL
## MUG CAKE

*Serves: 2  Prep time: 2 minutes  Cook time: 4 minutes*

Rich, warm, gooey cinnamon rolls are hard-to-resist breakfast treats. Traditionally baked cinnamon rolls are too time-consuming for most days, but a cinnamon roll mug cake can be thrown together in minutes. These are sweet and spicy, just like the real thing. Suddenly the thought of skipping breakfast becomes a thing of the past.

| | |
|---|---|
| ¼ cup butter, melted | ¼ teaspoon vanilla extract |
| ¼ cup brown sugar | ½ cup self-rising flour |
| 1 egg | Pinch baking soda |
| ¼ cup buttermilk | ¼ teaspoon ground cinnamon |

1. In a large measuring cup or medium bowl, mix together the butter, brown sugar, egg, buttermilk, and vanilla.

2. Add the flour, baking soda, and cinnamon, and stir *just* until blended.

3. Divide the batter between 2 mugs, being careful not to fill the mugs more than half full.

4. Microwave each cake for 1 to 2 minutes, or until firm but not overcooked.

   *Topping Suggestion:* Use Cream Cheese Frosting (page 158) to top this simple cinnamon roll. Spread it on while the cake is still hot, and sprinkle with chopped pecans.

   *Make It Gluten-Free:* Substitute gluten-free flour for the flour for a gluten-free version of this cake. Just remember to add an additional ⅛ teaspoon baking powder.

   *Variation:* Fold 2 tablespoons chopped pecans or raisins into the batter.

# BLUEBERRY CRUMB

MUG CAKE

*Serves: 2  **Prep time:** 2 minutes  **Cook time:** 4 minutes*

Here, ripe, juicy blueberries are enveloped in a sweet, buttery batter and topped with crunchy streusel. This coffee cake is summer in one perfect bite. You can add a few pecans to the batter if you like—they give it a little texture as well as flavor. If you happen to have a lemon on hand, grate a little of the peel into the batter, too. It brightens up the flavor and makes the sweetness of the blueberries really pop.

¼ cup butter, melted

¼ cup sugar

1 egg

¼ cup buttermilk

¼ teaspoon vanilla extract

½ cup self-rising flour

Pinch baking soda

¼ cup fresh blueberries

½ cup Streusel (page 164)

1.  In a large measuring cup or medium bowl, mix together the butter, sugar, egg, buttermilk, and vanilla.

2.  Add the flour and baking soda, and stir *just* until well blended.

3.  Fold the blueberries into the batter.

4.  Divide the batter between 2 mugs, being careful not to fill the mugs more than half full. Top each mug with ¼ cup streusel.

5.  Microwave each cake for 1 to 2 minutes, or until the cake is firm but not overcooked, and serve.

*Topping Suggestion:* Drizzling a little Vanilla Glaze (page 171) over the warm streusel gives a sweet finish to this coffee cake.

*Variation:* Raspberries or well-drained crushed pineapple work well in this cake, too.

# BANANA-NUT
## MUG CAKE

*Serves:* 2 *Prep time:* 2 *minutes* *Cook time:* 4 *minutes*

Banana-nut bread is to breakfast what macaroni and cheese is to dinner—pure comfort food. Try to get the ripest bananas possible. This recipe is also a great use for those old bananas that are past their prime and probably sitting on your counter right now! They are best and sweetest when they are almost liquefied. The bananas add both sweetness and moisture to this quick breakfast treat. Eat one for breakfast, and keep the second for an afternoon snack.

¼ cup butter, melted

1 very ripe banana, mashed

¼ cup sugar

1 egg

¼ cup buttermilk

½ cup self-rising flour

Pinch baking soda

¼ cup chopped pecans

1. In a large measuring cup or medium bowl, mix together the butter, banana, sugar, egg, and buttermilk.

2. Add the flour and baking soda, and stir *just* until well blended.

3. Fold the pecans into the batter.

4. Divide the batter between 2 mugs, being careful not to fill the mugs more than half full.

5. Microwave each cake for 1 to 2 minutes, or until the cake is firm but not overcooked, and serve.

*Topping Suggestion:* Banana-Nut Mug Cake is delicious topped with Praline Glaze (page 170).

*Make It Nut-Free:* This recipe easily becomes nut-free just by omitting the pecans. If you choose, fold chopped freeze-dried bananas into the batter to add a little crunch to the finished cake.

*Variation:* Use chopped walnuts instead of pecans. The sweetness of the banana pairs well with the bitterness of the walnuts.

# DOUGHNUT
## IN A MUG

*Serves: 2  Prep time: 2 minutes  Cook time: 4 minutes*

You can have doughnuts for breakfast without the mess of a deep fryer or making a trip to the doughnut shop. This cake has the flavor and texture of a cake doughnut without the greasiness of being fried. And what's a doughnut without a cup of hot coffee or a tall, cold glass of milk?

¼ cup butter, melted

¼ cup sugar

1 egg yolk

2 tablespoons milk

½ cup self-rising flour

¼ teaspoon ground nutmeg

1.  In a large measuring cup or medium bowl, mix together the butter, sugar, egg yolk, and milk.

2.  Add the flour and nutmeg, and stir *just* until well blended.

3.  Divide the batter between the 2 mugs, being careful not to fill the mugs more than halfway.

4.  Microwave each doughnut for 1 to 2 minutes, or until firm but not overcooked, and serve.

*Topping Suggestion:* You can glaze this "doughnut" with Vanilla Glaze (page 171) or just sprinkle the top with confectioners' sugar or cinnamon sugar.

*Variation:* Fold 2 tablespoons chopped apple pie filling into the batter for an apple fritter.

# MAPLE-BACON

MUG CAKE

*Serves: 2  **Prep time:** 2 minutes  **Cook time:** 4 minutes*

Maple and bacon—sweet and salty. It's like a having a pancake break-fast in one sweet bite. You can save a lot of time by buying precooked bacon or microwaving the bacon. You want it to be very crispy and easy to crumble. Drain it well on paper towels, or the fat will make the mug cake soggy. If this doesn't make your picky teenager eat break-fast, nothing will.

| | |
|---|---|
| ¼ cup butter, melted | ¼ cup milk |
| 2 tablespoons sugar | ½ cup self-rising flour |
| ¼ cup maple syrup | ¼ cup chopped, cooked bacon |
| 1 egg | |

1.  In a large measuring cup or medium bowl, mix together the butter, sugar, syrup, egg, and milk.

2.  Add the flour, and stir *just* until well blended.

3.  Fold the bacon into the batter.

4.  Divide the batter between 2 mugs, being careful not to fill the mugs more than half full.

5.  Microwave each cake for 1 to 2 minutes, or until the cake is firm but not overcooked, and serve.

    *Topping Suggestion:* If you spread Maple Frosting (page 161) on this cake while it's hot from the microwave, it will melt right into the cake—so good!

    *Make It Sugar-Free:* This recipe can be made sugar-free by using a sugar substitute for the maple syrup and adding ½ teaspoon maple flavoring.

    *Variation:* Substitute cooked, crumbled sausage for the bacon for an alternate (but equally satisfying) sweet-salty combination. Be sure to drain the sausage thoroughly of the grease.

# RASPBERRY-COFFEE CAKE

IN A MUG

*Serves: 2* **Prep time:** *2 minutes* **Cook time:** *4 minutes*

Lightly sweetened vanilla coffee cake with a ribbon of raspberry jam running through it makes this cake extra special. This works like a charm for serving a delightful birthday breakfast in bed. Substitute any jam you like for the raspberry in this recipe. Apricot jam? Out of this world. Peach marmalade? Just divine.

| | |
|---|---|
| ¼ cup butter, melted | ¼ cup sour cream |
| ¼ cup sugar | ½ cup self-rising flour |
| ½ teaspoon vanilla extract | Pinch baking soda |
| 1 egg | ¼ cup seedless raspberry jam, divided |

1. In a large measuring cup or medium bowl, mix together the butter, sugar, vanilla, egg, and sour cream.

2. Add the flour and baking soda, and stir *just* until well blended.

3. To each of 2 mugs, add 2 tablespoons of the batter followed by 2 tablespoons of the jam. Divide the remaining batter between the 2 mugs, being careful not to fill the mugs more than half full.

4. Microwave each cake for 1 to 2 minutes, or until the cake is firm but not overcooked, and serve.

   *Topping Suggestion:* A sweet Vanilla Glaze (page 171) makes this sweet coffee cake extra special.

   *Variation:* Add 3 tablespoons chopped almonds to the layers on top of the jam for a crunchy texture.

# OATMEAL-RAISIN
## MUG CAKE

*Serves: 2* **Prep time:** *2 minutes* **Cook time:** *4 minutes*

What's the secret to keeping raisins from sinking to the bottom of your mug cake? Give them a rough chop to help them stay evenly distributed throughout the batter. There's no need to chop them too finely, though. Aim for each raisin being cut into four pieces. Dried cranberries, dates, or figs work well in this cake, too. The flavor is wholesome and sweet—perfect for a busy morning.

| | |
|---|---|
| ¼ cup butter, melted | ¼ cup self-rising flour |
| ¼ cup brown sugar | ⅓ cup quick oats, uncooked |
| 1 egg | ¼ cup chopped raisins |
| ¼ cup milk | ½ cup Streusel (page 164), divided |

1.  In a large measuring cup or medium bowl, mix together the butter, brown sugar, egg, and milk.

2.  Add the flour, and stir *just* until well blended.

3.  Fold the oats and raisins into the batter.

4.  Divide the batter between 2 mugs, being careful not to fill the mugs more than halfway. Top each mug with ¼ cup of streusel.

5.  Microwave each cake for 1 to 2 minutes, or until firm but not overcooked, and serve.

    ***Topping Suggestion:*** Vanilla Glaze (page 171) can be drizzled over the cake if you like, but the streusel is a wonderful topping on its own.

    ***Make It Gluten-Free:*** Make this cake gluten-free by omitting the flour and using your favorite gluten-free flour instead. Almond flour is particularly nice and makes for a nice cake texture.

    ***Variation:*** Fold 2 tablespoons toasted coconut (see page 104) into the batter to make it like a baked granola muffin.

# CRUMB CAKE
## IN A MUG

*Serves: 2  Prep time: 2 minutes  Cook time: 4 minutes*

Crumb cake is a moist, sweet cake with a crunchy, crumbly topping. It makes a great breakfast or midmorning snack. The streusel topping is best when added in a thick layer to the top of the cake. Chopped pecans or walnuts can be mixed into the batter for more crunch, if you like.

¼ cup butter, melted

¼ cup sugar

1 egg

¼ cup vanilla Greek yogurt

½ cup self-rising flour

Pinch baking soda

½ cup Streusel (page 164), divided

1. In a large measuring cup or medium bowl, mix together the butter, sugar, egg, and yogurt.

2. Add the flour and baking soda, and stir *just* until well blended.

3. Divide the batter between 2 mugs, being careful not to fill the mugs more than half full. Top each liberally with ¼ cup of streusel.

4. Microwave each cake for 1 to 2 minutes, or until firm but not overcooked.

*Topping Suggestion:* Praline Glaze (page 170) is delicious spooned over the streusel.

*Variation:* Sprinkle blueberries or diced apples on top of the cake batter before adding the streusel topping. The burst of fruit flavor is a welcome addition.

# EASY PANCAKES AND BACON

*Serves: 2  Prep time: 2 minutes  Cook time: $1\frac{1}{2}$ minutes*

Pancakes and bacon are a leisurely weekend treat, but you can make them in a mug in a matter of minutes. Keep cooked bacon on hand and this recipe will come together lightening fast. Serve with a glass of orange juice and make any chaotic weekday morning a little more tolerable.

½ cup prepared pancake mix          ½ cup chopped, cooked bacon

¼ cup milk

1. In a small bowl, stir the milk and pancake mix together with a fork. Fold in the bacon.

2. Divide between two mugs.

3. Microwave for about $1\frac{1}{4}$ minutes or until top is firm but not overcooked.

4. Drizzle with warm maple syrup.

   *Topping Suggestion:* Maple syrup is classic, but you can use blueberry or apple pie filling as well.

   *Make It Gluten-Free:* Substitute your favorite gluten-free pancake mix.

   *Variation:* Fold in blueberries instead of bacon for a delicious blueberry pancake mug cake.

# 10

## *For the Grown-Ups*

Mudslide Mug Cake *123*

Rum Mug Cake *124*

Strawberry Margarita Mug Cake *125*

Spiked Mocha Mug Cake *126*

Bourbon and Cola Mug Cake *127*

Piña Colada Mug Cake *128*

Chocolate-Merlot Mug Cake *129*

Peach Daiquiri Mug Cake *130*

Grasshopper Mug Cake *131*

# RATED DELICIOUS FOR ADULTS

Alcohol can add a unique flavor variation to many different kinds of mug cakes. It doesn't take much, but it has a big impact on flavor. There are two ways to add the alcohol. You can use it as part of the liquid in the batter, or you can use it to soak the cake after baking. You may even want to do both.

Generally speaking, a lot of the actual alcohol evaporates during cooking, but not all of it. There's no reason a child couldn't have a piece of cake made with alcohol, as long as it has been baked in. Use your best discretion. Not much is needed to add flavor to the cake. A couple of tablespoons is just about right. If you're adding alcohol to a cake that doesn't call for it, you should decrease the other liquid by an equal amount.

Some delicious flavor combinations include:

## CHOCOLATE CAKE WITH

* Amaretto
* Coffee liqueur
* Crème de cacao
* Crème de menthe
* Dark Irish stout
* Irish cream
* Merlot

## YELLOW CAKE WITH

* Amaretto
* Bourbon
* Brandy
* Calvados
* Madeira
* Rum
* Sherry
* Triple Sec
* Whiskey

## WHITE CAKE WITH

* Amaretto
* Champagne
* White rum

You can add a sample-size bottle of alcohol to gift baskets for the perfect mug cake addition, or create a gift basket around a full-sized bottle.

A wine-themed basket might include a bottle of Merlot, the ingredients for the Chocolate-Merlot Mug Cake (page 129), some chocolate-covered cherries, and a couple of pretty shot glasses to go along with the mugs. It's a great combination for Valentine's Day.

The Mudslide Mug Cake (page 123) basket could include chocolate syrup, a couple of cocktail glasses, the mug cake mix with instructions, and a bottle each of coffee liqueur and Irish cream. These ingredients added to a chocolate-themed basket will really get the attention of any chocolate lover.

# MUDSLIDE

## MUG CAKE

*Serves: 2  **Prep time:** 2 minutes  **Cook time:** 4 minutes*

Coffee liqueur and Irish cream come together to create a classic mudslide cocktail, enjoyed here in a cake. If you'd like to make a non-alcoholic version, use Irish cream coffee creamer and strong, dark coffee in place of the Irish cream and coffee liqueurs.

| | |
|---|---|
| ¼ cup butter, melted | 2 tablespoons Irish cream liqueur |
| ½ cup sugar | 2 tablespoons coffee liqueur |
| 1 egg | ½ cup self-rising flour |

1. In a large measuring cup or medium bowl, mix together the butter, sugar, egg, Irish cream, and coffee liqueur.

2. Add the flour, and stir *just* until smooth.

3. Divide the batter between 2 mugs, being careful not to fill the mugs more than half full.

4. Microwave each cake for 2 minutes, or until the cake is firm but springy when lightly touched, and serve.

*Topping Suggestion:* Drizzle with warm Chocolate Ganache (page 162) to add some chocolatey goodness.

*Make It Gluten-Free:* Exchange the flour for your favorite gluten-free mix.

*Variation:* Fold ¼ cup bittersweet chocolate chips into the batter. The pockets of gooey chocolate make for a decadent cake texture.

# RUM

*Serves: 2  Prep time: 2 minutes  Cook time: 4 minutes*

This buttery, rich cake has rum baked right in. The alcohol evaporates during baking for a mellower rum flavor, but you can boost it back up with a sprinkle of your favorite rum on top of the finished cake. This mug cake is especially popular during the holiday season or after spending a day in the snow.

¼ cup butter, melted

½ cup sugar

1 egg

2 tablespoons milk

3 tablespoons dark or golden rum, divided

½ cup self-rising flour

1.  In a large measuring cup or medium bowl, mix together the butter, sugar, egg, milk, and 1 tablespoon of rum.

2.  Add the flour, and stir *just* until smooth.

3.  Divide the batter between 2 mugs, being careful not to fill the mugs more than half full.

4.  Microwave each cake for 2 minutes, or until the cake is firm but springy when lightly touched, and serve.

5.  Sprinkle each cake with 1 tablespoon of rum before serving.

*Topping Suggestion:* Spoon Rum Glaze (page 168) on this cake while it is still hot, and give it a minute to soak in.

*Variation:* For a deeper, smokier flavor, substitute bourbon or rye whiskey.

# STRAWBERRY MARGARITA

*Serves: 2  **Prep time:** 2 minutes  **Cook time:** 4 minutes*

Now you can have as much fun eating a strawberry margarita as you can drinking one. It is delicious served with fresh strawberries spooned over the top—especially when those berries are soaked in a little tequila. If you're making these for a party, it's fun to cook them in a jelly jar, then rub the jar rims with a little egg white or lemon juice and roll them in pink sugar crystals. Add a paper umbrella, and your guests will say Olé!

¼ cup coconut oil

¼ cup sugar

1 egg

2 tablespoons frozen strawberry
    margarita mix concentrate

1 tablespoon milk

3 tablespoons tequila, divided

½ cup self-rising flour

4–6 strawberries, cut into
    ¼-inch-thick slices

1.  In a small bowl, toss sliced strawberries with 2 tablespoons tequila. Set aside.

2.  In a large measuring cup or medium bowl, mix together the oil, sugar, egg, margarita mix, milk, and 1 tablespoon tequila.

3.  Add the flour, and stir *just* until smooth.

4.  Divide the batter between 2 mugs, being careful not to fill the mugs more than half full.

5.  Microwave each cake for 2 minutes, or until the cake is firm but springy when lightly touched, and serve, topped with strawberries.

    *Topping Suggestion:* A simple Vanilla Glaze (page 171) works well on this cake.

    *Make It Sugar-Free:* Use sugar-free margarita mix and your preferred sugar-free sweetener for a lighter version of this cake.

    *Variation:* Use any frozen cocktail mix in place of the strawberry margarita mix in this recipe for a variety of delicious flavor options.

# SPIKED MOCHA
MUG CAKE

*Serves: 2  Prep time: 2 minutes  Cook time: 4 minutes*

This is a deep chocolate cake with a generous splash of coffee liqueur. The combination of the chocolate and the coffee and cream flavor is a classic pairing. It's the perfect parental snack to unwind with after the kids' play date is over.

| | |
|---|---|
| ¼ cup butter, melted | 2 tablespoons milk |
| ½ cup sugar | 3 tablespoons self-rising flour |
| 1 egg | 2 tablespoons cocoa |
| 2 tablespoons coffee liqueur | ¼ cup mini chocolate chips |

1. In a large measuring cup or medium bowl, mix together the butter, sugar, egg, liqueur, and milk.

2. Add the flour and cocoa, and stir *just* until smooth.

3. Fold the chocolate chips into the batter.

4. Divide the batter between 2 mugs, being careful not to fill the mugs more than half full.

5. Microwave each cake for 2 minutes, or until the cake is firm but springy when lightly touched, and serve.

   *Topping Suggestion:* Chocolate Frosting (page 159) sprinkled with grated chocolate is a beautiful finish to this mug cake.

   *Variation:* Use Irish cream instead of coffee liqueur in this cake for a whiskey and cream flavor that also goes well with chocolate.

# BOURBON AND COLA

*Serves: 2  **Prep time:** 2 minutes  **Cook time:** 4 minutes*

Dad will revel in Father's Day with a bourbon and cola mug cake. His smile will grow even wider if the finished cake is drizzled with a little extra bourbon before serving. Kids can enjoy a classic cola cake by leaving the bourbon out and adding an extra tablespoon of milk.

| | |
|---|---|
| ¼ cup butter, melted | 2 tablespoons milk |
| ½ cup sugar | 1 tablespoon bourbon |
| 1 egg | 3 tablespoons self-rising flour |
| 2 tablespoons cola | 3 tablespoons cocoa |

1. In a large measuring cup or medium bowl, mix together the butter, sugar, egg, cola, milk, and bourbon.

2. Add the flour and cocoa, and stir *just* until blended.

3. Divide the batter between 2 mugs, being careful not to fill the mugs more than half full.

4. Microwave each cake for 2 minutes, or until the cake is firm but springy when lightly touched, and serve.

*Topping Suggestion:* Drizzle the cake with Chocolate Glaze (page 167) if desired.

*Make It Sugar-Free:* Make this cake sugar-free by substituting sugar-free sweetener like xylitol or Splenda for the sugar and using cola-flavored seltzer for the cola. You can also use diet cola, though many diet colas use aspartame, so check the label.

*Variation:* Make it a Cuba Libre by adding a squeeze of fresh lime and a tablespoon of grated lime zest to the batter.

# PIÑA COLADA

MUG CAKE

*Serves: 2  Prep time: 2 minutes  Cook time: 4 minutes*

A piña colada mug cake is a luscious mixture of coconut, pineapple, and rum that can make the dreariest day feel like a tropical vacation. Close your eyes and dream of warm breezes and salty ocean air. You can make this cake kid-friendly by leaving out the rum and using ½ teaspoon rum extract instead.

| | |
|---|---|
| ¼ cup butter, melted | ¼ cup piña colada mix |
| ½ cup sugar | 1 to 2 tablespoons rum |
| 1 egg | ½ cup self-rising flour |

1. In a large measuring cup or medium bowl, mix together the butter, sugar, egg, piña colada mix, and rum.

2. Add the flour, and stir *just* until blended.

3. Divide the batter between 2 mugs, being careful not to fill the mugs more than half full.

4. Microwave each cake for 2 minutes, or until the cake is firm but springy when lightly touched, and serve.

   *Topping Suggestion:* Rum Glaze (page 168) is delicious on this cake, especially when served with a scoop of vanilla ice cream.

   *Variation:* Use 1 tablespoon coconut flour in place of 1 tablespoon of the flour, and use cold coconut oil instead of butter for a more pronounced coconut flavor.

# CHOCOLATE-MERLOT
## MUG CAKE

*Serves: 2  **Prep time:** 2 minutes  **Cook time:** 4 minutes*

Merlot is a rich, fruity wine with a jammy, plum-and-honeysuckle flavor that pairs well with the chocolate in this very special mug cake. It smells and tastes very much like a fancy, jelly-filled European candy. This cake should be allowed to cool for a few minutes to let the flavor develop fully. For a prettier presentation, serve it with a small bunch of purple grapes alongside.

| | |
|---|---|
| ¼ cup butter, melted | 2 tablespoons Merlot |
| ½ cup sugar | ¼ cup self-rising flour |
| 1 egg | ¼ cup extra-dark cocoa |
| 2 tablespoons milk | |

1. In a large measuring cup or medium bowl, mix together the butter, sugar, egg, milk, and Merlot.

2. Add the flour and cocoa, and stir *just* until blended.

3. Divide the batter between 2 mugs, being careful not to fill the mugs more than half full.

4. Microwave each cake for 2 minutes, or until the cake is firm but springy when lightly touched, and let cool for 5 to 10 minutes before serving.

*Topping Suggestion:* Spoon warm Chocolate Ganache (page 162) over the top of this cake for a delicious, elegant dessert.

*Make It Vegan:* For a vegan version of this cake, use oil instead of the butter, leave out the egg and milk, and increase the Merlot to ¼ cup.

*Variation:* Fold 2 tablespoons bittersweet chocolate chips into the batter. Besides being delicious, it creates a silky texture.

# PEACH DAIQUIRI

*Serves: 2  **Prep time:** 2 minutes  **Cook time:** 4 minutes*

Sweet peach flavor and a kick of rum make this mug cake a wonderful summer dessert. If you want a bit more rum flavor, you can drizzle a little over the top of the cake just as it comes out of the microwave. This is delicious with a scoop of peach or vanilla ice cream served alongside or topped with some rum-soaked fresh peaches.

| | |
|---|---|
| ¼ cup butter, melted | 1 tablespoon dark rum |
| ½ cup sugar | 2 tablespoons milk |
| 1 egg | ½ cup self-rising flour |
| 2 tablespoons frozen peach daiquiri mix | |

1. In a large measuring cup or medium bowl, mix together the butter, sugar, egg, daiquiri mix, rum, and milk.

2. Add the flour, and stir *just* until blended.

3. Divide the batter between 2 mugs, being careful not to fill the mugs more than half full.

4. Microwave each cake for 2 minutes, or until the cake is firm but springy when lightly touched, and serve.

*Topping Suggestion:* Vanilla Glaze (page 171) works well on this cake.

*Variation:* Use strawberry daiquiri mix in place of the peach, and top with fresh strawberries for a completely different yet equally delicious option.

# GRASSHOPPER
## MUG CAKE

*Serves: 2 **Prep time:** 3 minutes **Cook time:** 4 minutes*

Mint and chocolate are one of the top combinations on the flavor spectrum. Here, crème de menthe and crème de cacao combine to make this mug cake a moist, chocolatey, minty delight. This cake is perfect for serving on Christmas Eve, when the kids are finally in bed and it's that magical moment for the adults to enjoy the calm before the chaos.

| | |
|---|---|
| ¼ cup butter | 2 tablespoons milk |
| 2 ounces bittersweet chocolate | 1 tablespoon crème de cacao |
| ½ cup sugar | 1 tablespoon crème de menthe |
| 1 egg | ¼ cup self-rising flour |

1. In a microwave-safe cup, melt the butter and the chocolate together in the microwave, stirring every few seconds until smooth.

2. In a medium bowl or large measuring cup, mix together the melted butter and chocolate, sugar, egg, milk, crème de cacao, and crème de menthe.

3. Add the flour, and stir *just* until blended.

4. Divide the batter between 2 mugs, being careful not to fill the mugs more than half full.

5. Microwave each cake for 2 minutes, or until the cake is firm but springy when lightly touched, and serve.

*Topping Suggestion:* Spoon warm Chocolate Ganache (page 162) over the cake before serving. Sprinkle crushed peppermint candies on top to give this cake a little extra pizzazz.

*Make It Gluten-Free:* Substitute gluten-free flour and add ⅛ teaspoon gluten-free baking powder.

*Variation:* If it's Girl Scout cookie season, you know it's time for their ubiquitous chocolate-covered mint cookies. Roughly chop a few, and fold 2 tablespoons of them into the cake batter for a minty, crunchy texture.

# 11

## *Mug Cakes for Special Diets*

Fat-Free Apple-Spice Mug Cake *135*

Low-Carb Chocolate Mug Cake *136*

Low-Carb Coconut Mug Cake *137*

Low-Calorie Mocha Mug Cake *138*

Paleo Banana Mug Cake *139*

Paleo Sweet Potato Mug Cake *140*

Whole-Food Oatmeal-Almond Mug Cake *141*

# HAVE YOUR CAKE AND EAT IT, TOO

Most mug cakes can be adapted to be low-calorie as well as appropriate for any special diet. In fact, many of the mug cakes in this book have suggestions for adapting the recipes for gluten-free, dairy-free, and other dietary needs. Chapter 2 provided suggestions for easy ingredient substitutions to make these recipes appropriate for most special diets.

Since mug cakes are so simple and quick to make, it will be hard to resist making them often. Here are 10 ways you can save calories and still enjoy your cake.

1. Substitute fat-free milk for whole milk.

2. Use fat-free sour cream or buttermilk in place of the milk in the recipe. Be sure to add a pinch of baking soda if you use one of these.

3. Use a low-cholesterol egg substitute in place of the eggs.

4. Use applesauce, prune purée in place of half the fat (which is usually butter or oil).

5. Use fat-free Greek yogurt in place of half the fat.

6. Use a measure-for-measure sugar substitute like Splenda or erythritol in place of the granulated or brown sugar.

7. Use half the amount of chocolate called for in the recipe.

8. Use 6 tablespoons cocoa, 1 tablespoon flavorless oil (such as vegetable or canola oil), and 1 tablespoon fat-free sour cream in place of 2 squares of unsweetened baking chocolate to save 90 calories.

9. Fat helps distribute the flavor in a cake, so when something is made lower fat, it can also mean lower flavor. Keep the same flavor by adding grated citrus rind, a few extra drops of vanilla, or an extra pinch of spice.

10. Flavored seltzers are a great zero-calorie substitute for liquids like milk or fruit juice. You can use them with the cakes to change their flavor. Try orange seltzer with a vanilla cake.

# FAT-FREE APPLE-SPICE

## MUG CAKE

*Serves: 2 **Prep time:** 2 minutes **Cook time:** 2 minutes*

This spicy apple mug cake has no added fat. The applesauce keeps this cake moist and gives it plenty of flavor. If you'd like to infuse more apple goodness into the cake, you can substitute unsweetened apple juice for the milk. Be sure to read labels and use unsweetened applesauce, or you'll add quite a few calories in the form of sugar added to sweetened applesauce. This cake is as guilt-free an after-school snack as you can provide.

½ cup unsweetened applesauce

2 tablespoons sugar

3 tablespoons nonfat milk

¼ teaspoon ground cinnamon

½ cup self-rising flour

1. In a large measuring cup or medium bowl, mix together the applesauce, sugar, and milk.

2. Add the cinnamon and flour, and stir *just* until smooth.

3. Divide the batter between 2 mugs, being careful not to fill the mugs more than half full.

4. Microwave each cake for 1 minute, or until the cake is firm but springy when lightly touched, and serve.

*Topping Suggestion:* Dust the top of the cake with confectioners' sugar.

*Make It Sugar-Free:* Substitute your preferred sugar-free sweetener.

*Variation:* Use ½ cup pumpkin purée in place of the applesauce for an equally moist, delicious cake.

# LOW-CARB CHOCOLATE
## MUG CAKE

*Serves: 2  Prep time: 2 minutes  Cook time: 3 minutes*

Chocolate cake on a low-carb diet? Why not? This cake will fulfill those chocolate cravings with just under 11 net carbohydrates per serving. It's perfect for those times when you just have to have something sweet. Adding 2 tablespoons of macadamia nuts adds less than 1 gram of carbohydrates and really increases the yum factor.

| | |
|---|---|
| ¼ cup butter, melted | 1 tablespoon coconut flour |
| ¼ cup sugar substitute | 2 tablespoons dark cocoa powder |
| 1 egg | ¼ teaspoon vanilla extract |
| 2 tablespoons almond flour | ½ teaspoon baking powder |

1.  In a large measuring cup or medium bowl, combine the butter, sugar substitute, egg, almond flour, coconut flour, dark cocoa powder, vanilla extract, and baking powder. Mix together until smooth.

2.  Divide the batter between 2 mugs, being careful not to fill the mugs more than half full.

3.  Microwave each cake for 1 to 1½ minutes, or until firm but springy when lightly touched, and serve.

*Topping Suggestion:* A generous spoonful of whipped cream sweetened with a little sugar-free sweetener is perfect on this decadent cake.

*Variation:* Fold a chopped, low-carb chocolate bar into the batter. Most have only 3 grams net carbs.

# LOW-CARB COCONUT
## MUG CAKE

*Serves: 2  Prep time: 2 minutes  Cook time: 4 minutes*

Cakes made with coconut flour tend to take longer to bake. This is because the coconut soaks up and holds the moisture in the cake. You'll likely need closer to 2 minutes, and maybe a little more, to microwave a mug cake with coconut flour in it. But this cake is worth those additional seconds. It has tons of coconut flavor and enough fiber to keep you satisfied for a long time.

¼ cup coconut oil, melted

¼ cup xylitol or erythritol

¼ teaspoon vanilla extract or coconut flavoring

2 tablespoons sour cream

2 tablespoons coconut milk

2 tablespoons coconut flour

3 tablespoons almond flour

¼ teaspoon baking soda

1.  In a large measuring cup or medium bowl, mix together the coconut oil, xylitol, vanilla, sour cream, coconut milk, coconut flour, almond flour, and baking soda.

2.  Divide the batter between 2 mugs, being careful not to fill the mugs more than half full.

3.  Microwave each cake for 2 minutes, or until the cake is firm but springy when lightly touched, and serve.

*Topping Suggestion:* Make your own crème fraiche with 1 tablespoon sour cream sweetened with a little sugar substitute. It is a perfect finish to this cake. The tangy sweetness and richness of the sour cream complements the sweet crumbliness of the cake.

*Make It Paleo:* Make this recipe Paleo-friendly by substituting raw honey for the sweeteners, using an additional ¼ cup coconut milk in place of the sour cream, and adding ¼ teaspoon freshly squeezed lemon juice.

*Variation:* Fold 2 tablespoons chopped macadamia nuts into the batter for a delightful crunch.

# LOW-CALORIE MOCHA
## MUG CAKE

*Serves: 2  Prep time: 2 minutes  Cook time: 3 minutes*

Enjoying this sweet, mocha mug cake when you're watching your calorie intake is one of life's little pleasures. It's so good that no one will know it's low-calorie if you don't tell them. It's a good way to let your kids enjoy snacks without worrying about junk food or too much sugar. Learning to eat healthy is something families have to do together, and this cake is a great place to start for lower-calorie desserts.

1 tablespoon butter, melted

¼ cup sugar substitute

1 egg white

½ cup self-rising flour

2 tablespoons cocoa powder

¼ cup cold, dark coffee

¼ teaspoon vanilla extract

1. In a large measuring cup or medium bowl, mix together the butter, sugar substitute, egg white, flour, cocoa powder, coffee, and vanilla.

2. Divide the batter between 2 mugs, being careful not to fill the mugs more than half full.

3. Microwave each cake for 1 to 1½ minutes, or until firm but springy when lightly touched, and serve.

*Topping Suggestion:* Greek vanilla yogurt is delicious on this cake. You can also use one of the low-fat, whipped chocolate yogurt varieties, if you like.

*Make It Vegan:* Omit the egg white and use coconut oil in place of the butter.

*Variation:* Try using a sugar-free chai mix in place of the cocoa and nonfat milk in place of the coffee for another coffeehouse flavor favorite.

# PALEO BANANA

*Serves: 2  Prep time: 2 minutes  Cook time: 2 minutes*

Paleo diet followers will love this banana cake. It's a fantastic way to treat yourself without falling off the wagon. Its sweet flavor means that the kids will love it, too. Since it's gluten-free, dairy-free, and low in fat, it can be enjoyed by nearly everyone. It's best served warm.

1 cup very ripe, mashed banana (about 2 bananas)

2 tablespoons raw honey

⅓ cup almond meal

½ teaspoon baking powder

2 tablespoons coconut oil

¼ cup chopped pecans

1. In a medium bowl, mix together the banana, honey, almond meal, baking powder, and coconut oil.

2. Fold the pecans into the batter.

3. Divide the batter between 2 mugs, being careful not to fill the mugs more than half full.

4. Microwave each cake for 1 minute, or until the cake is firm but springy when lightly touched, and serve.

*Topping Suggestion:* Sliced bananas or a drizzle of raw honey make for just the right finishing touch.

*Variation:* Fold 2 tablespoons chopped dates into the batter for a chewier cake texture.

# PALEO SWEET POTATO
## MUG CAKE

*Serves: 2  Prep time: 2 minutes  Cook time: 4 minutes*

Sweet and spicy, this mug cake is a delicious change of pace. Microwave a fresh sweet potato or yam for this one—canned sweet potato and yams almost always mean added sugar. Once microwaved, scoop out the sweet potato flesh, mash it, and you are ready to create this yummy, autumn-inspired cake. Not only are sweet potatoes naturally sweet, but they are full of important vitamins and minerals. Kids will love it, not realizing they're getting a vegetable in their dessert.

¼ cup coconut oil, melted

3 tablespoons raw honey

1 egg

1 cup sweet potato, cooked and mashed

⅓ cup almond flour

1 tablespoon coconut flour

1 teaspoon ground cinnamon

½ teaspoon baking powder

1. In a large measuring cup or medium bowl, mix together the coconut oil, honey, egg, and sweet potato.

2. Add the almond flour, coconut flour, cinnamon, and baking powder, and stir *just* until smooth.

3. Divide the batter between 2 mugs, being careful not to fill the mugs more than half full.

4. Microwave each cake for 2 minutes, or until the cake is firm but springy when lightly touched, and serve.

*Make It Low-Carb:* Substitute pumpkin purée for the sweet potato, using xylitol in place of the honey, and using butter instead of the coconut oil.

*Variation:* Use mashed acorn or Hubbard squash in place of the sweet potato.

# WHOLE-FOOD OATMEAL-ALMOND
## MUG CAKE

*Serves: 2  Prep time: 2 minutes  Cook time: 4 minutes*

A whole food is one that has not been overly processed. Whole grains, honey, maple syrup, nuts, and other ingredients are used in as close to a natural state as possible. This oatmeal-almond mug cake is wholesome and good for you and—just as important—delicious. The flavor is somewhat like granola, and it's full of vitamins, minerals, and fiber. Make your own self-rising whole-wheat flour by adding 1 teaspoon of baking powder to 1 cup minus 2 tablespoons whole-wheat flour.

2 tablespoons unsalted butter, melted

½ cup maple syrup

1 egg

¼ cup milk

¼ cup self-rising whole-wheat flour

¼ cup old-fashioned oats, ground in a blender

¼ cup almonds, chopped

1. In a large measuring cup or medium bowl, mix together the butter, syrup, egg, and milk.

2. Add the flour and oats, and mix *just* until smooth.

3. Fold the almonds into the batter.

4. Divide the batter between 2 mugs, being careful not to fill the mugs more than half full.

5. Microwave each cake for 2 minutes, or until the cake is firm but springy when lightly touched, and serve.

*Topping Suggestion:* Peeled and chopped apples, lightly sautéed in butter and sweetened with maple syrup, are wonderful with this cake.

*Make It Dairy-Free:* Use coconut oil instead of butter, and almond milk in place of the milk.

*Variation:* Add 1 tablespoon flaxseed meal for extra fiber. Fold 2 tablespoons of your favorite dried fruit into the batter for a little chewiness and an extra kick of flavor.

# 12

## *Beyond Cakes*

Cheesecake in a Mug *145*

Sugar Cookie in a Mug *146*

Chocolate Chip Cookie in a Mug *147*

Chocolate Cobbler in a Mug *148*

Apple Crisp in a Mug *149*

Peach Cobbler in a Mug *150*

Pumpkin Pie in a Mug *151*

Chocolate Pudding in a Mug *152*

Ham and Cheese Mug Quiche *153*

# SAVORY MUG TREATS

You don't have to limit yourself to dessert when it comes to recipes in a mug. Savory meals in a mug are just as fun to make and can be a lifesaver when it comes to getting the kids to eat something easy after school. Here's a recipe for macaroni and cheese to give you a head start.

## MACARONI AND CHEESE IN A MUG

*Serves 1*  **Prep time:** *1 minute*  **Cook time:** *$2\frac{1}{2}$ minutes*

½ cup elbow uncooked macaroni

½ cup milk

½ cup finely shredded sharp cheddar cheese

1.  In a 20-ounce mug, microwave the macaroni and milk for 1 minute. Stir, and microwave for 1 more minute. Stir again, and microwave a final 30 more seconds, or until the pasta is cooked.

2.  Add the cheese to the mug, stir until the cheese is melted and the macaroni is coated, and serve.

### VARIATION

If you're watching your carbs, you can make this mac and cheese with half cream, half water, and use cauliflower in place of the pasta.

### ADD-INS

Try 2 to 3 tablespoons of the following ingredients to make your mac and cheese totally drool-worthy. Whatever you use should be added at the same time as the cheese.

Canned chiles

Cooked ground beef

Cooked, chopped broccoli

Cooked, crumbled bacon

Diced tomatoes

Sautéed onion

Other seasonings can be added for even more flavor. Try a pinch of any of these (add them at the same time as the cheese):

Ground cayenne

Ground chipotle

Ground nutmeg

Mustard powder

Smoked paprika

Taco seasoning

# CHEESECAKE

*Serves: 2  Prep time: 2 minutes  Cook time: 5 minutes  Total time: 1 hour 5 minutes*

It takes hours to make a cheesecake, right? Not with this mug version. This is another great dessert that's perfect for trying out different flavor combinations. The crust alone can be made with almost any type of cookie. Just crush the cookies to make crumbs—let the kids have at this one. Everyone can create their own signature cheesecake.

¼ cup graham cracker crumbs

1 tablespoon butter, melted

¼ cup confectioners' sugar

¼ cup sour cream

⅓ cup cream cheese, at room temperature

1 egg, beaten

¼ teaspoon vanilla extract

1. Grease the inside of 2 mugs.

2. In a small bowl, mix together the graham cracker crumbs and melted butter. It will be moist but crumbly.

3. Divide the crust between each mug, and press the mixture down to cover the entire bottom of each mug.

4. In a large measuring cup or medium bowl, mix together the confectioners' sugar, sour cream, cream cheese, egg, and vanilla.

5. Divide the cheesecake mixture between the 2 mugs, being careful not to fill the mugs more than half full.

6. Microwave each cheesecake for 1 minute. Let each rest for about 5 seconds, and then microwave for another 20 seconds. Repeat the resting and microwaving one more time. For the best texture, let the cheesecake chill in the refrigerator for 1 hour.

*Topping Suggestion:* Spoon your favorite fruit topping over the cheesecake before serving.

*Variation:* Stir 1 tablespoon chopped pecans, chopped chocolate sandwich cookies, or chocolate chips into the cheesecake mixture, or mix in 1 tablespoon peanut butter, melted bittersweet chocolate, or fruit purée.

# SUGAR COOKIE

*Serves: 2  **Prep time:** 2 minutes  **Cook time:** 1½ minutes*

A sugar cookie is pure comfort food. When you cook this in a wider mug, it takes less time and is more cookielike than when made in a narrower mug. Be sure to eat this cookie warm—the texture changes as it cools. Adjust the amount of vanilla to suit your personal tastes. It's fun to add a tablespoon or two of colored sprinkles to the batter.

| | |
|---|---|
| 2 tablespoons unsalted butter, melted | 1 egg |
| 3 tablespoons sugar | ⅓ cup self-rising flour |
| ½ teaspoon vanilla extract | 1 tablespoon colored sugar crystals, divided |

1. Grease the inside of 2 mugs.

2. In a medium bowl, mix together the butter, sugar, vanilla, egg, and flour.

3. Divide the cookie dough between the mugs, being careful not to fill the mugs more than half full, and sprinkle ½ tablespoon of colored sugar crystals on top of each.

4. Microwave each cookie for 45 seconds, or until a toothpick inserted in the center comes out clean. Eat while still warm.

   *Topping Suggestion:* Spread some food-color-tinted Vanilla Frosting (page 157) onto the cookies and top with sprinkles.

   *Variation:* Use brown sugar instead of white sugar for a hint of butterscotch flavor.

# CHOCOLATE CHIP COOKIE

IN A MUG

*Serves: 2  Prep time: 2 minutes  Cook time: 1 minute*

Chocolate chip cookies are not only delicious—they make the entire house smell good. The next time you have bored kids on a chilly, rainy afternoon, suggest making these and eat them while playing a favorite board game. When cooked in a mug, the cookies are a little more cakelike.

2 tablespoons unsalted butter, melted

2 tablespoons granulated sugar

2 tablespoons firmly packed brown sugar

1 teaspoon vanilla extract

1 egg

⅓ cup self-rising flour

¼ cup mini chocolate chips

2 tablespoons chopped pecans

1. In a medium bowl, mix together the butter, granulated sugar, brown sugar, vanilla, and egg.

2. Add the flour and stir *just* until well mixed.

3. Fold the chocolate chips and pecans into the dough.

4. Divide the dough between 2 mugs, being careful not to fill the mugs more than half full.

5. Microwave each cookie for 30 seconds. Let rest for about 5 seconds. The cookie will continue to cook while it cools. If it still isn't done, microwave it for 10 seconds more, and serve.

*Topping Suggestion:* Add a scoop of vanilla ice cream and drizzle with hot fudge sauce before serving.

*Make It Gluten-Free:* Don't let gluten sensitivity keep anyone from this fun treat. Substitute 1 tablespoon coconut flour, 2 tablespoons almond flour, and 3 tablespoons brown rice flour for the regular flour. Add a pinch of baking soda, too.

*Variation:* Fold 2 tablespoons peanut butter chips into the dough, too. Make chocolate chocolate-chip cookies by using ¼ cup self-rising flour and 2 tablespoons cocoa.

# CHOCOLATE COBBLER

IN A MUG

*Serves: 2  Prep time: 2 minutes  Cook time: 1 minute*

This is a great dessert for kids to help make. There are enough steps to allow everyone to have a part. Let one person mix the batter while another blends the cocoa and sugar for the topping. Yet another person can sprinkle the topping onto the batter. But an adult should be the one to add the boiling water. The cobbler comes out moist and chocolatey with a warm, chocolate pudding sauce underneath.

| | |
|---|---|
| 3 tablespoons self-rising flour | ¼ cup milk |
| 5 tablespoons sugar, divided | 2 tablespoons milk chocolate chips |
| 4 tablespoons cocoa, divided | 3 tablespoons boiling water or coffee, divided |

1.  In a medium bowl or large measuring cup, mix the flour, 3 tablespoons of sugar, 3 tablespoons of cocoa, and the milk.

2.  Fold the chocolate chips into the batter.

3.  Divide the batter between 2 mugs, being careful not to fill the mugs more than half full.

4.  In a small bowl, mix together the remaining 1 tablespoon of cocoa and 2 tablespoons of sugar. Sprinkle evenly on top of the batter in each mug.

5.  Pour 1½ tablespoons boiling water or coffee into each mug.

6.  Microwave each cobbler for 30 seconds. The finished result should be firm with a thick sauce underneath.

7.  Serve hot, or refrigerate for a midnight snack.

*Topping Suggestion:* Add a dollop of whipped cream dusted with a little cocoa powder to the top of the cobbler.

*Variation:* Make this with chopped peanut butter cups in place of the chocolate chips for a burst of creamy peanut butter–chocolate flavor.

# APPLE CRISP

*Serves: 2  Prep time: 2 minutes  Cook time: 2 minutes  Total time: 12 minutes*

This is a great recipe for young cooks to make, especially if you use apple pie filling. Kids like to get their hands into things, and this crisp topping is best when mixed with the fingers. Make sure an older child or adult is around to supervise, though. The filling can get very hot.

1 cup apple, peeled and cut into thin slices, or 1 cup apple pie filling

¼ cup quick oats

½ cup all-purpose flour

2 tablespoons brown sugar

1 tablespoon granulated sugar

1 teaspoon ground cinnamon

Pinch salt

3 tablespoons unsalted butter, melted

1.  In a small, covered bowl, microwave the apple slices for 1 minute. If using apple pie filling, skip this step.

2.  Divide the apples between 2 mugs, being careful not to fill the mugs more than half full.

3.  In a medium bowl, combine the oats, flour, brown sugar, granulated sugar, cinnamon, salt, and butter, blending until the mixture looks crumbly. Using your fingers works best.

4.  Divide the mixture in half, and sprinkle on top of the apples in each mug.

5.  Microwave each crisp for 1 minute. Allow to cool for 5 minutes before eating.

*Topping Suggestion:* A frosty scoop of vanilla bean ice cream is a classic way to finish this dish. Whipped cream is delicious, too.

*Make It Sugar-Free:* Substitute 1 tablespoon xylitol and 2 tablespoons brown sugar substitute for the white and brown sugars.

*Variation:* Use fresh, ripe peaches or peach pie filling for a taste of summer.

# PEACH COBBLER

*Serves: 2  Prep time: 2 minutes  Cook time: 4 minutes*

Juicy peaches and a tender biscuit topping make this peach cobbler just right for any occasion. It's actually pretty healthy, so surprise the family by serving this for breakfast on a Monday morning. If that doesn't get the week off to a great start, nothing will. Any fruit can be substituted for the peaches. Make this with your seasonal favorite.

½ cup sliced peaches

¼ cup sugar, divided

½ cup biscuit mix

2 tablespoons milk

1.  In a medium bowl, mix the peaches and 2 tablespoons of sugar.

2.  Divide this mixture between 2 mugs, being careful not to fill the mugs more than half full.

3.  In the same bowl, mix together the biscuit mix, the remaining 2 tablespoons of sugar, and the milk until it forms a thick dough.

4.  Drop the dough by teaspoons over the peaches in each mug.

5.  Microwave each cobbler for 1½ to 2 minutes, or until the dough is firm and the fruit is bubbly, and serve.

*Topping Suggestion:* Vanilla ice cream on a warm peach cobbler is unbeatable, but whipped cream works just as well.

*Variation:* Apple pie filling is a good substitute for the peach in this recipe. Try ¼ cup sliced strawberries and ¼ cup rhubarb. You'll just need to cook the rhubarb first.

# PUMPKIN PIE
## IN A MUG

*Serves: 2  Prep time: 2 minutes  Cook time: 6 minutes  Total time: 11 minutes*

Pumpkin pie doesn't have to be just a seasonal dessert. This smooth, rich pumpkin pie can be had anytime you want. What about starting a tradition of making this for the first frost of the season? Throwing a winter-in-July party? Eyes will widen with delight when you serve this.

¼ cup vanilla wafer crumbs

1 tablespoon unsalted butter, melted

⅔ cup pumpkin purée

1 egg

2 tablespoons evaporated milk

¼ cup brown sugar

1½ teaspoons pumpkin pie spice

1. In a small bowl, mix together the wafer crumbs and the butter. Divide the mixture between 2 mugs, and press it into the bottom of each to make a crust.

2. In a medium bowl, mix together the pumpkin purée, egg, evaporated milk, brown sugar, and pumpkin pie spice.

3. Divide the pie filling between each mug, being careful not to fill the mugs more than half full.

4. Microwave each pie for 2 to 3 minutes, or until a knife inserted into the center of the filling comes out clean. Let each pie cool for 5 minutes before serving.

*Topping Suggestion:* Top with a generous spoonful of whipped cream. Grate a little bit of fresh nutmeg over the whipped cream if you like.

*Make It Gluten-Free:* Use a gluten-free cookie for the crumb crust, or leave the crust out entirely for more of a pumpkin custard.

*Variation:* Use acorn squash, Hubbard squash, or sweet potato for the pumpkin purée. Make the crust with gingersnap or graham cracker crumbs in place of the vanilla wafer crumbs.

# CHOCOLATE PUDDING

*Serves: 2  Prep time: 2 minutes  Cook time: 4 minutes*

Forget about instant pudding mixes. This creamy chocolate pudding is just as quick—or quicker—and the flavor and texture are so much better. You can adjust the intensity of the chocolate flavor in this by using different kinds of chocolate, or even mixing several varieties to give it the exact chocolate taste you're looking for.

1 cup milk, divided

⅓ cup milk chocolate chips or bittersweet chocolate chips, divided

2 tablespoons sugar

1 tablespoon plus 1 teaspoon cornstarch

1 tablespoon unsalted butter, melted

¼ teaspoon vanilla extract

Pinch salt

1. Divide the milk and chocolate chips between 2 mugs, being careful not to fill the mugs more than half full. Microwave each for 1 minute. Stir the mixture until smooth.

2. In a small bowl, mix together the sugar, cornstarch, butter, vanilla, and salt. Divide this mixture between each mug. Stir until the contents of both mugs are well mixed, ensuring that there are no lumps.

3. Microwave each pudding for 30 seconds, give it a stir, and microwave it for an additional 15 seconds. Continue stirring and microwaving until the pudding is thick, and serve.

*Topping Suggestion:* A big spoonful of whipped cream is perfect over this dessert. Make it even fancier by adding grated chocolate on top of the cream.

*Make It Dairy-Free:* Use coconut milk in place of the milk and coconut oil for the butter.

*Variation:* Omit the chocolate and double the vanilla for vanilla pudding. For butterscotch pudding, use brown sugar instead of white, add an additional 1 tablespoon unsalted butter, and omit the chocolate chips.

# HAM AND CHEESE QUICHE

## IN A MUG

*Serves: 2  **Prep time:** 2 minutes  **Cook time:** 1 minute*

Quiche is a luxurious breakfast or brunch, but few people have the time to get up and put a quiche on the table on a busy weekday. Well, now you can. This recipe has everything: ham, cheese, creamy eggs, and a delicious crust. Plus, you will have it on the table before the coffee finishes brewing. A wide coffee cup, rather than a tall mug, works best for this recipe.

2 thin slices French bread baguette

2 eggs

3 tablespoons half and half cream

1 tablespoon cream cheese cut in small pieces

2 tablespoons chopped ham

2 tablespoons shredded Swiss cheese

1. Beat the eggs and cream together with a fork. Add salt and pepper to taste.

2. Cut the bread into small cubes and place in the bottom of each coffee cup.

3. Sprinkle the cream cheese, ham, and Swiss on top.

4. Pour the egg mixture into the cup.

5. Microwave until done, about 1 minute each.

6. Let stand a few seconds to firm up before serving.

*Topping Suggestion:* Sprinkle a few chopped chives on the top for a quick garnish.

*Make It Low-Fat:* Use egg replacer, fat-free half and half cream, fat-free cream cheese, and low-fat Swiss cheese.

*Variation:* Add a tablespoon of drained, canned chiles and substitute Cheddar for the Swiss cheese for a Southwestern variation.

# 13

## *Frostings, Toppings, and Glazes*

Vanilla Frosting *157*

Cream Cheese
Frosting *158*

Chocolate Frosting *159*

Peanut Butter
Frosting *160*

Maple Frosting *161*

Chocolate Ganache *162*

Bourbon
Caramel Syrup *163*

Streusel *164*

Salted Caramel
Sauce *165*

Lemon Curd *166*

Chocolate Glaze *167*

Rum Glaze *168*

Lemon Glaze *169*

Praline Glaze *170*

Vanilla Glaze *171*

# THE ART OF DECORATING WITH FONDANT

Fondant is an edible, firm sugar paste that allows you to create all kinds of fun finishes for your mug cakes and other desserts. Think of it as edible Play-Doh—you can roll it out to cover a cake; use a knife or small cutters to create letters, numbers, and shapes; or form it into flowers and figures. The possibilities are endless. Commercial fondant looks fantastic, but its flavor is not to everyone's liking. Luckily, it's quite simple to make your own fondant that is as delicious as it is pretty.

## EASY HOMEMADE MARSHMALLOW FONDANT

*Makes 2¼ pounds* **Prep time:** *15 minutes, plus overnight for refrigerating*
**Cook time:** *45 seconds*

¼ cup unsalted butter, softened

16 ounces miniature marshmallows

¼ cup water

1 teaspoon clear vanilla extract

2 pounds of confectioners' sugar, divided

1.  Put the butter in a large bowl and set it aside.

2.  In a large bowl, microwave the marshmallows for 30 seconds on high. They should begin to melt. Microwave for another few seconds at a time to melt them completely. Keep a close eye on them so they don't begin to burn.

3.  Stir the water and the vanilla into the melted marshmallows, stirring until the mixture is smooth.

4.  Beat in the confectioners' sugar 1 cup at a time until a sticky dough forms. Reserve 1 cup of the sugar for kneading the fondant. The dough will be stiff.

5.  Dust a clean surface with confectioners' sugar. Rub the butter over your hands to knead the fondant. Turn the fondant out onto the surface, and knead it until it is smooth and easy to work with. It will lose its stickiness. This will take about 10 minutes.

6.  Form your fondant into a ball, wrap it tightly, and refrigerate overnight.

TO USE:

Allow the fondant to come to room temperature. Dust a surface with confectioners' sugar, and roll out the fondant.

# VANILLA FROSTING

*Makes: 2 servings  Prep time: 2 minutes*

Vanilla frosting goes well on every kind of cake. It's creamy and sweet but won't overpower the most delicate flavors. The trick to this is to make sure that the butter is at room temperature, or softened enough to make it easy to mix in with the sugar and vanilla. Rather than trying to spread this on the cake, make a drift of frosting with a spoon.

**3 tablespoons butter, softened**

**¼ cup confectioners' sugar, plus additional as needed**

**¼ teaspoon vanilla extract**

In a small bowl, mix together the butter, confectioners' sugar, and vanilla. If the frosting is too thin, add more confectioners' sugar until you achieve the right texture.

*Make It Vegan:* You can make this frosting vegan by using cold coconut oil instead of butter. Coconut oil liquefies at room temperature, so you'll need to keep it refrigerated.

# CREAM CHEESE FROSTING

*Makes: 2 servings  Prep time: 2 minutes*

If you're making a spice, red velvet, or other cake you have to have a good cream cheese frosting to go with, this recipe will do the trick. Easily made by hand, this frosting is a balance of sweet and tangy perfection. It will sit like a cloud atop your cake.

3 tablespoons cream cheese, softened

¼ cup confectioners' sugar, plus additional if needed

¼ teaspoon vanilla extract

2 drops freshly squeezed lemon juice

In a small bowl, mix together the cream cheese, sugar, vanilla, and lemon juice. If the frosting is too thin, add more confectioners' sugar until the right texture is achieved.

*Variation:* Use ½ teaspoon orange juice instead of the vanilla to add a citrus note to the frosting.

# CHOCOLATE FROSTING

*Makes:* 2 *servings* **Prep time:** 2 *minutes*

Chocolate cake with a creamy chocolate frosting is one of the most popular desserts ever conceived. This frosting stays creamy and is very chocolatey. Using a dark cocoa instead of regular cocoa will give it even more chocolate flavor and a darker color. With this the kids will beg to lick the spoon.

3 tablespoons butter, salted or unsalted, softened

¼ cup confectioners' sugar

1 tablespoon cocoa

¼ teaspoon vanilla

1 teaspoon milk (if needed)

Mix together the butter, confectioners' sugar, cocoa, and vanilla in a small bowl. If the texture is too thick, add the milk to achieve the right texture.

*Make It Dairy-Free:* For a dairy-free version of this cake, use peanut butter instead of butter and substitute any milk you wish. This version goes especially well on the Chocolate–Peanut Butter Mug Cake (page 52).

*Variation:* Instead of using milk to thin the frosting, you can use cold, black coffee.

# PEANUT BUTTER FROSTING

*Makes: 2 servings  Prep time: 2 minutes*

Peanut butter frosting is good on chocolate cake and is an unexpected delight when used on banana cake. Sweet and salty, this creamy frosting is one you'll use again and again. A sprinkle of chopped peanuts and mini chocolate chips on a frosted cake will delight everyone.

2 tablespoons butter, softened

1 tablespoon creamy peanut butter

¼ cup confectioners' sugar, plus additional if needed

¼ teaspoon vanilla extract

In a small bowl, mix together the butter, peanut butter, sugar, and vanilla. Add more confectioners' sugar to achieve the right texture, if necessary.

*Variation:* In the case of a peanut allergy, you can use sunflower seed butter, cashew butter, or almond butter in place of the peanut butter. Diligently check the label to make sure it isn't processed in a facility that processes peanuts. For a bolder flavor, add 1 teaspoon honey or molasses. You may have to add a little more confectioners' sugar to thicken the texture of the frosting.

# MAPLE FROSTING

*Makes:* 2 servings  *Prep time:* 2 minutes

Maple flavor is unlike any other. It's important to use real maple syrup and not maple-flavored syrup in this frosting. Real maple syrup comes in different grades, but they are not all available in all parts of the country. You'll get the most flavor with a Grade B syrup, if you have a choice.

3 tablespoons butter, softened

⅓ cup confectioners' sugar, plus additional if needed

¼ teaspoon vanilla extract

1 tablespoon maple syrup

In a small bowl, mix together the butter, sugar, vanilla, and maple syrup. Add more confectioners' sugar to achieve the right texture, if necessary.

*Make It Dairy-Free:* Make this frosting dairy-free by using cold coconut oil in place of the butter.

*Variation:* Fold chopped walnuts into this frosting to give it more texture.

# CHOCOLATE GANACHE

*Makes: ⅔ cup  Prep time: 2 minutes  Cook time: 1 minute*

Ganache is a shiny, rich chocolate sauce that can be used to top a variety of desserts. When chilled, it becomes firm, and you can make chocolate truffles out of it, too. Although it is beautiful and looks complicated, it really is one of the easiest toppings to make. It's important that water does not get into the chocolate, however— you'll end up with a mess. This is especially good on the Doughnut in a Mug (page 114). Refrigerate any leftover ganache for up to one week.

½ cup heavy cream

¼ cup bittersweet, semisweet, or milk chocolate chips, or a combination of chips

1. In a small bowl, microwave the cream until it comes *just* to a boil.

2. Add the chocolate chips to the bowl, and stir until the chocolate is smooth and shiny.

   *Variation:* Once the chocolate is melted, you can add a tablespoon of liqueur or flavoring to give it more depth of flavor.

# BOURBON CARAMEL SYRUP

*Makes: 1¼ cups  Prep time: 2 minutes  Cook time: 4 minutes*

Homemade caramel syrup is easier than you think. This is rich and creamy with the mellow flavor of bourbon whiskey—it isn't for the kiddos. It is a delicious addition to nearly any of the cakes in this book, and it makes a delicious and thoughtful gift. The sauce will last for about a month in the refrigerator. Keep it tightly covered.

¼ cup unsalted butter, melted

1 cup brown sugar

½ cup heavy cream

1 tablespoon bourbon whiskey

1.  In a medium, microwave-safe bowl, mix together the butter, brown sugar, and cream.

2.  Microwave for 2 minutes. Stir carefully and thoroughly, and then microwave for another 2 minutes, or until it thickens.

3.  Stir in the whiskey. Use the syrup hot or refrigerate it. If refrigerated, warm it before using.

    *Variation:* Use rum instead of the whiskey for a more subtle flavor of caramel sauce. Or make this recipe family-friendly by leaving out the whiskey and adding 1 teaspoon vanilla extract.

# STREUSEL

*Makes: 2 servings  Prep time: 2 minutes*

Streusel is a crumbly mixture of sugar, flour, and butter with a hint of cinnamon. Sometimes ginger, nutmeg, and cloves are added as well. Streusel is always added to the top of the cake before it is cooked. It works best if you mix the butter into the flour and sugar mixture with your fingers just until it becomes crumbly. It's a great one to let the kids put together.

2 tablespoons butter, cold

3 tablespoons all-purpose flour

¼ cup brown sugar

Pinch ground cinnamon

In a small bowl, mix together the butter, flour, brown sugar, and cinnamon.

*Substitution Tip:* Use your favorite brown sugar substitute in place of the brown sugar.

*Variation:* Add in 2 tablespoons finely chopped pecans or walnuts for more texture.

# SALTED CARAMEL SAUCE

*Makes: 1¼ cups*  **Prep time:** *2 minutes*  **Cook time:** *4 minutes*

Salt helps bring out the flavors in food and balance the sweetness in baked goods. Use this sauce warm or cold on the mug cake of your choice. Extra sauce need never go to waste. Spoon it over ice cream for an unexpected treat. It's especially good on the Chocolate Chip Cookie in a Mug (page 147).

| | |
|---|---|
| ¼ cup salted butter, melted | ½ cup heavy cream |
| 1 cup brown sugar | 1 teaspoon kosher salt |

1. In a medium, microwave-safe bowl, mix together the butter, brown sugar, cream, and salt.

2. Microwave for 2 minutes. Stir the sauce carefully and thoroughly, and then microwave it another 2 minutes, or until it thickens.

   *Variation:* Mix in crushed toffee candy when the caramel has cooled to add some texture and a delicious flavor.

# LEMON CURD

*Makes: 1 cup  Prep time: 2 minutes  Cook time: 5 minutes*

Lemon curd is a tangy, fresh spread that makes a lovely topping for any cake that needs a little brightening. It also can be used as a delicious filling and is wonderful on toast, too. It can be kept tightly covered in the refrigerator for up to two weeks.

½ cup granulated sugar

2 egg yolks

½ cup freshly squeezed lemon juice

¼ cup unsalted butter, softened

1. In a small bowl, mix together the sugar, egg yolks, and lemon juice.

2. Microwave for 1 minute at a time, stirring after every minute, until the mixture is thick and clings to a spoon, about 5 minutes.

3. Remove the curd from the microwave, and stir in the butter.

*Variation:* Any citrus will work well in this recipe. Try orange, lime, grapefruit, or a combination of juices.

# CHOCOLATE GLAZE

*Makes: $\frac{3}{4}$ cup*  **Prep time:** *2 minutes*  **Cook time:** *3 minutes*

This is a thin, chocolate glaze with a shiny sheen. The key to making it is to whisk the ingredients together as smooth as possible before microwaving them. It's good on ice cream, too. A great variation is to make a hard shell topping for ice cream—use coconut oil instead of butter, and water instead of milk.

½ cup sugar

¼ cup cocoa

2 tablespoons milk or water

2 tablespoons butter, softened

¼ teaspoon vanilla extract

1.  In a small, microwave-safe bowl, whisk together the sugar, cocoa, milk, and butter until smooth and well blended.

2.  Microwave until it comes to a boil, about 2 minutes. Stir thoroughly and microwave again until it thickens slightly, about 1 more minute.

3.  Remove the glaze from the microwave, and stir in the vanilla.

*Make It Vegan:* You can make this glaze vegan by using water instead of milk and substituting cold coconut oil for the butter.

*Variation:* If you'd like mocha flavor, use cold, black coffee instead of the milk or water.

# RUM GLAZE

*Makes: 2 servings  Prep time: 2 minutes*

Glazes should be very thin. They are typically spooned over a cake while it is still hot. This allows the glaze to soak into the cake, adding even more flavor and moisture. A glaze is the quickest, easiest way to top a mug cake and is especially good when you have a very flavorful cake that doesn't need much to finish it. This rum glaze is delicious on the Yellow Mug Cake (page 39) as well as on many others in this book.

1 tablespoon butter, melted

¼ cup confectioners' sugar, plus additional if needed

1 tablespoon rum

In a small bowl, mix together the butter, sugar, and rum. It should be thin, but not watery. Add more confectioners' sugar to achieve the right texture, if necessary.

*Make It Vegan:* Make a vegan version of this glaze by substituting cold coconut oil for the butter.

*Variation:* Use coconut rum instead of plain rum—it gives the glaze a tropical flavor.

# LEMON GLAZE

*Makes: 2 servings  Prep time: 2 minutes*

Lemon glaze is a must for the lemon mug cake as well as any of the fruit mug cakes. It adds a tangy punch to anything you spoon it on. When spread on a hot cake, the glaze will melt a little, and as it cools, it will create a delicately crispy glaze. For even more lemony goodness, grate some lemon peel over the top of your glazed cake before serving.

1 tablespoon unsalted butter, melted

¼ cup confectioners' sugar, plus additional if needed

1 tablespoon freshly squeezed lemon juice

In a small bowl, mix together the butter, sugar, and lemon juice. If the glaze is too thin, add more confectioners' sugar to achieve the right texture.

*Make It Vegan:* Make it vegan by using cold coconut oil instead of the butter. The coconut oil will give it a faint coconut flavor, which goes great with lemon.

*Variation:* Use freshly squeezed lime juice in place of the lemon juice to change the flavor a little. The lime juice variation works well with the Cherry Limeade Mug Cake (page 73).

# PRALINE GLAZE

*Makes: 2 servings* **Prep time:** *2 minutes* **Cook time:** *2 minutes*

The secret to the praline glaze is getting the brown sugar melted into the butter without overcooking it. Stir the brown sugar and butter mixture often while it cooks. Take it out of the microwave as soon as the mixture is blended and smooth. Even overcooking it by a few seconds could ruin it. You may not need all the confectioners' sugar called for.

**3 tablespoons butter, melted**

**2 tablespoons brown sugar**

**¼ cup confectioners' sugar**

**¼ teaspoon vanilla extract**

1. In a small, microwave-safe bowl, mix together the butter and brown sugar. Microwave until the brown sugar dissolves, about 2 minutes, stirring often.

2. Stir in the confectioners' sugar, a little at a time, until the glaze is smooth and at the consistency you want.

3. Stir in the vanilla.

*Variation:* Add butternut or hazelnut flavoring in place of the vanilla extract to give the praline glaze a slightly nuttier flavor.

# VANILLA GLAZE

*Makes:* 2 *servings* **Prep time:** 2 *minutes*

The delicate flavor of a vanilla glaze won't overwhelm anything it is used on. For a nutty flavor to the glaze, use a brown butter. Make this by melting the butter on the stove in a small pot until it turns a golden brown color. It's not really possible to brown butter in the microwave. Watch it carefully because it burns easily. Use it just like the regular melted butter in this recipe.

2 tablespoons butter, salted or unsalted, melted

¼ cup confectioners' sugar, plus additional if needed

½ teaspoon vanilla extract

¼ teaspoon milk (if needed)

In a small bowl, mix together the butter, confectioners' sugar, and vanilla. Add more confectioners' sugar or a few drops of milk to achieve the right texture, if necessary.

*Make It Vegan:* Make this glaze vegan by using cold coconut oil instead of butter, and substitute almond or coconut milk.

*Variation:* A teaspoon of your favorite liqueur adds additional flavor depths to this glaze.

# Common Food Substitutions

## BAKING POWDER

Baking powder helps the batter rise. Most baking powder is double-acting—which means that it begins to work when liquids are added, and then gets an extra burst of energy when it is heated. To substitute for a teaspoon of baking powder, use:

* ¼ teaspoon baking soda, plus ½ teaspoon cream of tartar.

* ¼ teaspoon baking soda, plus ½ cup buttermilk. Decrease the liquid in the recipe by ½ cup.

* ¼ teaspoon baking soda, plus 1 tablespoon freshly squeezed lemon juice or vinegar.

## BROWN SUGAR

Brown sugar is simply sugar with a little molasses added back in. It is moist and should be packed down firmly for measuring.

To substitute for 1 cup brown sugar, use:

* 1 cup white sugar, plus ¼ cup molasses. Decrease the liquid in the recipe by ¼ cup.

* 1 cup white sugar, plus ¼ cup maple syrup. Decrease the liquid in the recipe by ¼ cup.

* 1 cup white sugar.

* 1¼ cup confectioners' sugar.

## BUTTER

There are various reasons you may not want to use butter. Coconut oil is the preferred substitute for butter in most of these recipes. Be sure to get organic, unrefined extra-virgin coconut oil, because the commercial versions are too highly processed and will not add the delicate texture and flavor of the organic type.

Substitute in equal measure:

* Coconut oil

* Margarine

* Oil

* Shortening

## BUTTERMILK

Traditional buttermilk is the liquid left in the churn after butter is made, but modern commercial buttermilk is just milk with a culture added, much like yogurt. The culture causes it to be slightly acidic, adding flavor and improving the texture of your cake. Sour cream or yogurt will work best as substitutes, but in a pinch you can use any of these other options.

To substitute for 1 cup of buttermilk, use:

* 1 cup yogurt

* 1 cup sour cream

* 1 tablespoon freshly squeezed lemon juice, plus enough milk to make 1 cup total liquid

* 1 tablespoon vinegar, plus enough milk to make 1 cup total liquid

## COCOA AND CHOCOLATE

If you use cocoa as a substitute for chocolate, it is important that you add butter or other extra fat or your dish will be too dry. There are several kinds of cocoa, but you'll most often see Dutch process or extra-dark cocoas in your grocery store. You can use them interchangeably, depending on whether you prefer dark chocolate or a lighter chocolate flavor. You can also use milk, dark, semisweet, bittersweet, and white chocolate interchangeably in equal measures.

* For ¼ cup cocoa, use 1 ounce unsweetened chocolate.

* For 1 ounce unsweetened chocolate, use 3 tablespoons cocoa and 1 tablespoon butter.

* For 1 ounce semisweet chocolate, use 3 tablespoons cocoa, 1 tablespoon butter, and 4 teaspoons sugar OR 1 ounce unsweetened chocolate, 4 teaspoons sugar, and 1 tablespoon butter.

* For 1 ounce bittersweet chocolate, use 1 (1-ounce) square of unsweetened chocolate plus 4 teaspoons sugar OR 1 ounce semisweet chocolate chips plus 1 teaspoon shortening.

## EGGS

All the recipes in this book were tested with large grade A free-range, organic eggs. Eggs give batters a richer texture and help them rise high and light. Since you are working with such small amounts of ingredients when making a mug cake, the cakes can get spongy and "eggy." This is why each recipe is designed to make two cakes. If you find a recipe seems to have too much egg, try leaving the egg out completely and see if you like it better. You can also substitute 2 egg yolks or 2 egg whites for one whole egg, if you wish. The texture will be richer (in the case of the yolks) or lighter (in the case of the egg whites), depending on which you use.

To substitute for 1 egg, use:

* ¼ cup silken tofu

* 3 tablespoons mayonnaise

* Half a banana, pureed with ½ teaspoon baking powder

* 1 tablespoon powdered flaxseed soaked in 3 tablespoons water

* Egg substitute, as directed on the package

## FLOUR

The recipes in this book were made with the homemade self-rising flour recipe given in the beginning of the book. When flour is called for, it means self-rising flour unless another flour is specified. Cake flour has little protein, so it results in a tenderer product, but you should be aware that different manufacturers create flours with varying degrees of protein. It's best to try several brands of flour to see which you like best.

* 1 cup cake flour equals 1 cup all-purpose flour, minus 2 tablespoons.

* 1 cup self-rising flour equals $\frac{7}{8}$ cup all-purpose flour, $1\frac{1}{2}$ teaspoons baking powder, and $\frac{1}{2}$ teaspoon salt.

* 1 cup self-rising flour equals 1 cup cake flour, $1\frac{1}{2}$ teaspoons baking powder, and $\frac{1}{2}$ teaspoon salt.

* 1 cup gluten-free flour equals 1 cup all-purpose flour.

## LEMON JUICE

Lemon juice is an acid that helps foods rise and adds flavor. While you can substitute vinegar for lemon juice, it won't work if the lemon juice is giving the cake flavor rather than just acidity. Always use lime, grapefruit, or orange juice as a substitute if the cake is citrus flavored.

To substitute for 1 teaspoon freshly squeezed lemon juice, use:

* $\frac{1}{2}$ teaspoon vinegar

* 1 teaspoon white wine

* 1 teaspoon lime, grapefruit, or orange juice

## MILK

Milk helps keep the cake crumb tender. It's best not to use a fat-free milk unless the recipe calls for it. In most cases, any of the following liquids can be substituted for milk in the recipe.

To substitute for 1 cup of milk, use:

* 1 cup soy milk

* 1 cup goat milk

* 1 cup rice milk

* 1 cup coconut milk

* 1 cup almond milk

* 1 cup water

* 1 cup juice

* $\frac{2}{3}$ cup evaporated milk, plus $\frac{1}{3}$ cup water

* $\frac{1}{4}$ cup dry milk powder, plus 1 cup water

# Measurement Conversions

## Volume Equivalents (Liquid)

| US STANDARD | US STANDARD (OUNCES) | METRIC (APPROXIMATE) |
|---|---|---|
| 2 tablespoons | 1 fl. oz. | 30 mL |
| ¼ cup | 2 fl. oz. | 60 mL |
| ½ cup | 4 fl. oz. | 120 mL |
| 1 cup | 8 fl. oz. | 240 mL |
| 1½ cups | 12 fl. oz. | 355 mL |
| 2 cups or 1 pint | 16 fl. oz. | 475 mL |
| 4 cups or 1 quart | 32 fl. oz. | 1 L |
| 1 gallon | 128 fl. oz. | 4 L |

## Volume Equivalents (Dry)

| US STANDARD | METRIC (APPROXIMATE) |
|---|---|
| ⅛ teaspoon | 0.5 mL |
| ¼ teaspoon | 1 mL |
| ½ teaspoon | 2 mL |
| ¾ teaspoon | 4 mL |
| 1 teaspoon | 5 mL |
| 1 tablespoon | 15 mL |
| ¼ cup | 59 mL |
| ⅓ cup | 79 mL |
| ½ cup | 118 mL |
| ⅔ cup | 156 mL |
| ¾ cup | 177 mL |
| 1 cup | 235 mL |
| 2 cups or 1 pint | 475 mL |
| 3 cups | 700 mL |
| 4 cups or 1 quart | 1 L |
| ½ gallon | 2 L |
| 1 gallon | 4 L |

## Oven Temperatures

| FAHRENHEIT (F) | CELSIUS (C) (APPROXIMATE) |
|---|---|
| 250° | 120° |
| 300° | 150° |
| 325° | 165° |
| 350° | 180° |
| 375° | 190° |
| 400° | 200° |
| 425° | 220° |
| 450° | 230° |

## Weight Equivalents

| US STANDARD | METRIC (APPROXIMATE) |
|---|---|
| ½ ounce | 15 g |
| 1 ounce | 30 g |
| 2 ounces | 60 g |
| 4 ounces | 115 g |
| 8 ounces | 225 g |
| 12 ounces | 340 g |
| 16 ounces or 1 pound | 455 g |

# Sources for Ingredients

While you'll be able to find all the ingredients used in the recipes at most large grocery stores, some smaller chains do not carry the specialty ingredients necessary in gluten-free baking. If you have Whole Foods, Trader Joe's, or Sprouts near you, they are good sources for these flours. Any of the flours and ingredients you can't find locally can be ordered at the following online stores:

* Amazon.com

* Guistos, Giustos.com

* King Arthur Flour, kingarthurflour.com

# References

...........................

Gluten-Free Girl. "How to Make All-Purpose Gluten-free Flour Mix." Accessed December 8, 2014. glutenfreegirl.com/2012/07 /how-to-make-a-gluten-free-all-purpose-flour-mix/.

The Atkins Diet. "Phase 2: Balance Your Diet." Accessed December 16, 2014. http://www.atkins.com/how-it-works/atkins-20/phase-2.

The Paleo Diet. "Getting Real about Paleo: Quantifying Hunter Gatherer Food Choices." Accessed December, 15, 2014. thepaleodiet.com/getting-real-paleo-quantifying-hunter-gatherer -food-choices.

# Index

................

## A

Almond flour, 25
  Low-Carb Coconut
    Mug Cake, 137
  Paleo Sweet Potato
    Mug Cake, 140
  Pound Cake in a Mug, 43
Almond milk, 11, 21
Almonds
  Whole-Food Oatmeal-
    Almond Mug Cake, 141
Amaretto, 122
Apple Crisp in a Mug, 149
Apple pie filling
  Apple Crisp in a Mug, 149
  Caramel Apple Mug Cake, 75
Applesauce
  Applesauce Mug Cake, 65
  Caramel Apple Mug Cake, 75
Aspartame, 21

## B

Bacon
  Easy Pancakes and Bacon
    Mug Cakes, 119
  Maple-Bacon Mug Cake, 115
Baking powder, substitutions
    for, 173
Bananas
  Banana-Chocolate-Peanut
    Butter Mug Cake, 64
  Banana Mug Cake, 63
  Banana-Nut Mug Cake, 113
  Classic Banana Split, 32
  Hummingbird Mug Cake, 106
  Paleo Banana Mug Cake, 139
Basic Chocolate Mug
    Cake, 27–28
Basic Mug Cake, 26
Basics, 9–10
Beyond cakes, 144–153
  Apple Crisp in a Mug, 149
  Cheesecake in a Mug, 145
  Chocolate Chip Cookie
    in a Mug, 147

Chocolate Cobbler
    in a Mug, 148
Chocolate Pudding
    in a Mug, 152
Ham and Cheese Quiche
    in a Mug, 153
Peach Cobbler in a Mug, 150
Pumpkin Pie in a Mug, 151
Sugar Cookie in a Mug, 146
Birthdays, 82–93
  Butterscotch Mug Cake, 90
  Chocolate Chip Mug Cake, 86
  Chocolate Confetti
    Mug Cake, 84
  Chocolate Fudge
    Mug Cake, 87
  Confetti Mug Cake, 83
  Mocha Mug Cake, 85
  Pink Cherry Mug Cake, 92
  Rainbow Mug Cake, 88–89
  Salted Caramel Mug Cake, 93
  White Wedding Cake
    in a Mug, 91
Biscuit mix
  Peach Cobbler in a Mug, 150
Bittersweet chocolate
  Grasshopper Mug Cake, 131
Blueberries
  Blueberry Crumb
    Mug Cake, 112
  Blueberry-White Chocolate
    Mug Cake, 61
  Lemon-Blueberry
    Mug Cake, 60
  Red, White, and Blue
    Mug Cake, 105
Bourbon, 122
  Bourbon and Cola
    Mug Cake, 127
  Bourbon Caramel Syrup, 163
Brandy, 122
Breakfast, 110–119
  Banana-Nut Mug Cake, 113
  Blueberry Crumb
    Mug Cake, 112

Cinnamon Roll Mug Cake, 111
Crumb Cake in a Mug, 118
Doughnut in a Mug, 114
Easy Pancakes and Bacon
    Mug Cake, 119
Maple-Bacon Mug Cake, 115
Oatmeal-Raisin Mug Cake, 117
Raspberry-Coffee Cake
    in a Mug, 116
weekend mug cake, 110
Brown rice flour, 20
Brown sugar, 14
  substitutions for, 173
Butter, 11
  substitutions for, 173–174
  unsalted, 15
Buttercream frosting, 29
Butterfinger candy bars
  Holy Cow! Mug Cake, 54–55
Buttermilk, 11
  substitutions for, 174
Butterscotch Mug Cake, 90

## C

Cake flour, 11
Calvados, 122
Caramel Apple Mug Cake, 75
Caramel Mug Cake, 35
Caramel syrup
  Classic Banana Split, 32
Carrot Cake in a Mug, 40
Chai tea bags
  Vanilla Chai Mug Cake, 99
Champagne, 122
Cheesecake in a Mug, 145
Cherries. See Maraschino
    cherries
Cherry-Chocolate Chip
    Mug Cake, 62
Cherry Limeade Mug Cake, 73
Chocolate, 46–55
  Chocolate-Mint Mug Cake, 53
  Chocolate-Peanut Butter
    Mug Cake, 52
  Chocolate-Pecan
    Mug Cake, 50

German Chocolate Mug Cake, 51
Gooey Chocolate Mug Cake, 48
Holy Cow! Mug Cake, 54–55
Homemade Vegan Cocoa Chips or Chunks, 46
Lava Mug Cake, 47
Mexican Chocolate Mug Cake, 49
substitutions for, 174–175
Chocolate cake, adding liquors to, 122
Chocolate chips, 24
Banana-Chocolate-Peanut Butter Mug Cake, 64
Cherry-Chocolate Chip Mug Cake, 62
Chocolate Chip Cookie in a Mug, 147
Chocolate Cobbler in a Mug, 148
Chocolate-Covered Cherry Mug Cake, 103
Chocolate Ganache, 162
Chocolate Pudding in a Mug, 152
Spiked Mocha Mug Cake, 126
Chocolate Chip Mug Cake, 86
Chocolate Cobbler in a Mug, 148
Chocolate-Covered Cherry Mug Cake, 103
Chocolate Frosting, 159
Chocolate Ganache, 162
Chocolate Glaze, 167
Chocolate ice cream Classic Banana Split, 32
Chocolate-Merlot Mug Cake, 129
Chocolate Pudding in a Mug, 152
Cinnamon Roll Mug Cake, 111
Classics, 32–43
Caramel Mug Cake, 35
Carrot Cake in a Mug, 40
Classic Banana Split, 32
Devil's Food Mug Cake, 36
Lemon Mug Cake, 37
Marble Mug Cake, 38
Pineapple Upside-Down Mug Cake, 41–42
Pound Cake in a Mug, 43

Spice Mug Cake, 34
Vanilla Mug Cake, 33
Yellow Mug Cake, 39
Clementine Mug Cake, 78
Cocoa, Devil's Food Mug Cake, 36
Basic Chocolate Mud Cake, 27–28
Bourbon and Cola Mug Cake, 127
Chocolate Cobbler in a Mug, 148
Chocolate Confetti Mug Cake, 84
Chocolate-Covered Cherry Mug Cake, 103
Chocolate Frosting, 159
Chocolate Fudge Mug Cake, 87
Chocolate Glaze, 167
Chocolate-Merlot Mug Cake, 129
Chocolate-Mint Mug Cake, 53
Chocolate-Peanut Butter Mug Cake, 52
Chocolate-Pecan Mug Cake, 50
Gooey Chocolate Mug Cake, 48
Holy Cow! Mug Cake, 54–55
Lava Mug Cake, 47
Low-Calorie Mocha, 138
Marble Mug Cake, 38
Mexican Chocolate Mug Cake, 49
Red Velvet Mug Cake, 102
Spiked Mocha Mug Cake, 126
substitutions for, 174–175
Coconut
Coconut Mug Cake, 71
German Chocolate Mug Cake, 51
Pineapple-Coconut Mug Cake, 104
Coconut flour, 22, 25
Low-Carb Coconut Mug Cake, 137
Paleo Sweet Potato Mug Cake, 140
Coconut milk, 11, 21, 25
Low-Carb Coconut Mug Cake, 137
Coconut oil, 21

Coffee
Low-Calorie Mocha, 138
Coffee liqueur, 122
Mudslide Mug Cake, 123
Spiked Mocha Mug Cake, 126
Cola
Bourbon and Cola Mug Cake, 127
Confetti Mug Cake, 83
Cream, 25
Bourbon Caramel Syrup, 163
Cream cheese
Cheesecake in a Mug, 145
Cream Cheese Frosting, 158
Crème de cacao, 122
Grasshopper Mug Cake, 131
Crème de menthe, 122
Grasshopper Mug Cake, 131
Crumb Cake in a Mug, 118

D

Daiquiri mix
Peach Daiquiri Mug Cake, 130
Dairy-free, 21
Dark chocolate
Lava Mug Cake, 47
Dark Irish stout, 122
Date sugar, 14
Devil's Food Mug Cake, 36
Dietary substitution tricks, 20
Diet soda, 21
Doughnut in a Mug, 114
Dried fruit, 24

E

Earl Grey and Lemon Mug Cake, 79
Easy Homemade Marshmallow Fondant, 156
Easy Pancakes and Bacon Mug Cake, 119
Eggnog Mug Cake, 100
Eggs, 11
substitutions for, 175
Erythritol, 20, 21

F

Fall, fruit availability in, 58, 70
Fat-Free Apple-Spice Mug Cake, 135
Flour, 10–11
substitutions for, 175–176
Fondant, decorating with, 156

Food coloring
   Rainbow Mug Cake, 88–89
   Red Velvet Mug Cake, 102
Food substitutions, 173–177
French bread baguette
   Ham and Cheese Quiche
     in a Mug, 153
Frostings, toppings, and
   glazes, 155–171
   Bourbon Caramel
     Syrup, 163
   Chocolate Frosting, 159
   Chocolate Ganache, 162
   Chocolate Glaze, 167
   Cream Cheese Frosting, 158
   Lemon Curd, 166
   Lemon Glaze, 169
   Maple Frosting, 161
   Peanut Butter Frosting, 160
   Praline Glaze, 170
   Rum Glaze, 168
   Salted Caramel Sauce, 165
   Streusel, 164
   Vanilla Frosting, 157
   Vanilla Glaze, 171
Fruits. See also specific
   dried, 24
   seasonal, 58, 70
Fruit toppings, 29
Fruity cakes, 57–67
   Applesauce Mug Cake, 65
   Banana-Chocolate-Peanut
     Butter Mug Cake, 64
   Banana Mug Cake, 63
   Blueberry-White Chocolate
     Mug Cake, 61
   Cherry-Chocolate Chip
     Mug Cake, 62
   Key Lime Mug Cake, 66
   Lemon-Blueberry
     Mug Cake, 60
   Strawberry Shortcake
     in a Mug, 59
   White Chocolate-Raspberry
     Mug Cake, 67

G

German's Sweet Chocolate
   German Chocolate
     Mug Cake, 51
Gingerbread Mug Cake, 77
Glazes. See Frostings,
   toppings, and glazes

Gluten-free, 20
Gluten-free flour, 20
Gluten-free, self-rising
   flour mixes, 22–23
   making your own, 22–23
Grasshopper Mug Cake, 131
Greek yogurt
   Crumb Cake in a Mug, 118
Grown-ups, 122–131
   Bourbon and Cola
     Mug Cake, 127
   Chocolate-Merlot
     Mug Cake, 129
   Grasshopper Mug Cake, 131
   Mudslide Mug Cake, 123
   Peach Daiquiri Mug Cake, 130
   Piña Colada Mug Cake, 128
   Rum Mug Cake, 124
   Spiked Mocha Mug Cake, 126
   Strawberry Margarita
     Mug Cake, 125

H

Ham and Cheese Quiche
   in a Mug, 153
Holidays, 95–107
   Chocolate-Covered Cherry
     Mug Cake, 103
   Eggnog Mug Cake, 100
   Hot Chocolate and
     Marshallow Mug Cake, 97
   Hummingbird Mug Cake, 106
   Irish Cream Mug Cake, 107
   Pineapple-Coconut
     Mug Cake, 104
   Pumpkin Spice and
     Chipotle Mug Cake, 101
   Red Velvet Mug Cake, 102
   Red, White, and Blue
     Mug Cake, 105
   Vanilla Chai Mug Cake, 99
   White Chocolate-Peppermint
     Mug Cake, 98
Honey, 14, 24
   Paleo Banana Mug Cake, 139
   Paleo Sweet Potato
     Mug Cake, 140
Hot Chocolate and Marshallow
   Mug Cake, 97
Hot fudge syrup
   Classic Banana Split, 32
Hummingbird Mug Cake, 106

I

Ingredients, 10–14
   sources for, 179
Irish cream, 122
   Irish Cream Mug Cake, 107
   Mudslide Mug Cake, 123

K

Key Lime Mug Cake, 66
Kosher salt, 14

L

Lemonade drink mix
   Pink Lemonade Mug Cake, 74
Lemon juice, substitutions
   for, 176
Lemons
   Lemon-Blueberry
     Mug Cake, 60
   Lemon Curd, 166
   Lemon Glaze, 169
   Lemon Mug Cake, 37
Limeade concentrate
   Cherry Limeade
     Mug Cake, 73
Liquors. See also specific
   chocolate cakes with, 122
   white cakes with, 122
   yellow cakes with, 122
Low-Calorie Mocha
   Mug Cake, 138
Low-carb, 25
Low-Carb Chocolate
   Mug Cake, 136
Low-Carb Coconut
   Mug Cake, 137
Low-carb substitutes, 22

M

Macaroni and Cheese
   in a Mug, 144
Madeira, 122
Maple-Bacon Mug Cake, 115
Maple Frosting, 161
Maple-Nut Mug Cake, 72
Maple syrup, 14
   Maple-Bacon Mug Cake, 115
   Maple Frosting, 161
   Maple-Nut Mug Cake, 72
   Whole-Food Oatmeal-
     Almond Mug Cake, 141
Maraschino cherries/juice
   Cherry-Chocolate Chip
     Mug Cake, 62

Cherry Limeade
  Mug Cake, 73
Chocolate-Covered Cherry
  Mug Cake, 103
Classic Banana Split, 32
Pineapple Upside-Down
  Mug Cake, 41–42
Pink Cherry Mug Cake, 92
Marble Mug Cake, 38
Margarita mix
  Strawberry Margarita
    Mug Cake, 125
Marshmallows
  Easy Homemade Marsh-
    mallow Fondant, 156
  Hot Chocolate and
    Marshmallow
    Mug Cake, 97
Measurement conversions, 178
Merlot, 122
  Chocolate-Merlot
    Mug Cake, 129
Microwave ovens, 12–13
Milk, 11
  substitutions for, 176–177
Milk chocolate
  Hot Chocolate and Marsh-
    mallow Mug Cake, 97
  Lava Mug Cake, 47
Milk chocolate chips
  Gooey Chocolate
    Mug Cake, 48
Mint extract
  Chocolate-Mint
    Mug Cake, 53
Mocha Mug Cake, 85
Mudslide Mug Cake, 123
Mug cake party, 82
Mug cakes
  as addictive, 7
  baking in oven, 19–20
  basics for, 9–10
  giving as gift, 96
  ingredients for, 10–14
  making your first, 12
  making your own, 25
  tips and tricks, 14–16
  transforming, 32
  troubleshooting, 17
Mugs, 12

N
Nut-free, 24
Nuts. See Almonds;
    Pecans; Walnuts

O
Oatmeal-Raisin Mug Cake, 117
Oats
  Apple Crisp in a Mug, 149
  Oatmeal-Raisin Mug Cake, 117
  Whole-Food Oatmeal-
    Almond Mug Cake, 141
Oven, baking mug cake
  in, 19–20

P
Paleo Banana Mug Cake, 139
Paleo Sweet Potato
  Mug Cake, 140
Pancake mix
  Easy Pancakes and Bacon
    Mug Cake, 119
Peach Cobbler in a Mug, 150
Peach Daiquiri Mug Cake, 130
Peanut butter
  Banana-Chocolate-Peanut
    Butter Mug Cake, 64
  Chocolate-Peanut Butter
    Mug Cake, 52
  Peanut Butter Frosting, 160
Peanut butter cups
  Chocolate-Peanut Butter
    Mug Cake, 52
Pecans
  Banana Mug Cake, 63
  Banana-Nut Mug Cake, 113
  Chocolate Chip Cookie
    in a Mug, 147
  Chocolate-Pecan
    Mug Cake, 50
  Classic Banana Split, 32
  German Chocolate
    Mug Cake, 51
  Hummingbird Mug Cake, 106
  Paleo Banana Mug Cake, 139
Peppermint candy
  White Chocolate-Peppermint
    Mug Cake, 98
Piña colada mix
  Piña Colada Mug Cake, 128
  Pineapple-Coconut
    Mug Cake, 104

Pineapple/pineapple juice
  Carrot Cake in a Mug, 40
  Hummingbird Mug Cake, 106
  Pineapple-Coconut
    Mug Cake, 104
  Pineapple Upside-Down
    Mug Cake, 41–42
Pink Cherry Mug Cake, 92
Pink Himalayan sea salt, 14
Pink Lemonade Mug Cake, 74
Potato starch, 20
Pound Cake in a Mug, 43
Praline Glaze, 170
Pumpkin Mug Cake, 76
Pumpkin Pie in a Mug, 151
Pumpkin seeds, 24
Pumpkin Spice and Chipotle
  Mug Cake, 101

R
Rainbow Mug Cake, 88
Raisins
  Oatmeal-Raisin Mug Cake, 117
Raspberries
  Raspberry-Coffee Cake
    in a Mug, 116
  White Chocolate-Raspberry
    Mug Cake, 67
Red Velvet Mug Cake, 102
Red, White, and Blue
  Mug Cake, 105
Rice milk, 11, 21
Rum, 122
  Eggnog Mug Cake, 100
  Peach Daiquiri Mug Cake, 130
  Piña Colada Mug Cake, 128
  Rum Glaze, 168
  Rum Mug Cake, 124

S
Salt, 14
Salted Caramel Sauce, 165
  Caramel Apple Mug Cake, 75
  German Chocolate
    Mug Cake, 51
  Holy Cow! Mug Cake, 54–55
  Salted Caramel Mug Cake, 93
Savory Mug Treats, 144
Sea salt, 14
Seasonal Favorites, 69–79
  Caramel Apple Mug Cake, 75

Cherry Limeade
  Mug Cake, 73
Clementine Mug Cake, 78
Coconut Mug Cake, 71
Earl Grey and Lemon
  Mug Cake, 79
Gingerbread Mug Cake, 77
Maple-Nut Mug Cake, 72
Pink Lemonade Mug Cake, 74
Pumpkin Mug Cake, 76
Seasonal fruits, 58, 70
Self-rising flour, 10–11
Sherry, 122
Sour cream, 25
  Cheesecake in a Mug, 145
  Low-Carb Coconut
    Mug Cake, 137
Soy butter, 21, 24
Soy milk, 11, 21
Special Diets, 133–141
  Fat-Free Apple-Spice
    Mug Cake, 135
  Low Calorie Mocha
    Mug Cake, 138
  Low-Carb Chocolate
    Mug Cake, 136
  Low-Carb Coconut
    Mug Cake, 137
  Paleo Banana Mug Cake, 139
  Paleo Sweet Potato
    Mug Cake, 140
  Whole-Food Oatmeal-
    Almond Mug Cake, 141
Spice Mug Cake, 34
Spiked Mocha Mug Cake, 126
Spring, fruit availability
  in, 58, 70
Stevia, 20, 21, 25
Strawberries
  Classic Banana Split, 32
  Red, White, and Blue
    Mug Cake, 105

Strawberry Margarita
  Mug Cake, 125
Strawberry Shortcake
  in a Mug, 59
Strawberry ice cream
  Classic Banana Split, 32
Strawberry syrup
  Classic Banana Split, 32
Streusel, 164
  Blueberry Crumb
    Mug Cake, 112
  Crumb Cake in a Mug, 118
  Oatmeal-Raisin Mug Cake, 117
Sucralose, 21
Sugar, 14
Sugar Cookie in a Mug, 146
Sugar-free, 20–21
Sugar substitutes, 25
Summer, fruit availability
  in, 58, 70
Sunflower seeds, 24
Sweet potatoes
  Paleo Sweet Potato
    Mug Cake, 140
Swiss cheese
  Ham and Cheese Quiche
    in a Mug, 153

T
Tahini, 24
Tapioca flour, 20
Tequila
  Strawberry Margarita
    Mug Cake, 125
Textured vegetable protein
  granules, 24
Tips and tricks, 14–16
Toasted marshmallow, 29
Toppings, 16. See also Frostings,
  toppings, and glazes
Trial run, 13
Triple Sec, 122
Troubleshooting, 17

U
Unsalted butter, 15

V
Vanilla Chai Mug Cake, 99
Vanilla Frosting, 157
Vanilla Glaze, 171
Vanilla ice cream
  Classic Banana Split, 32
Vanilla Mug Cake, 33
Vegan, 24

W
Walnuts
  Carrot Cake in a Mug, 40
  Maple-Nut Mug Cake, 72
Whipped cream, 25, 29
  Classic Banana Split, 32
Whiskey, 122
White cakes with liquors, 122
White chocolate
  White Chocolate-Peppermint
    Mug Cake, 98
White chocolate chips
  Blueberry-White Chocolate
    Mug Cake, 61
  White Chocolate-Raspberry
    Mug Cake, 67
White granulated sugar, 14
White Wedding Cake
  in a Mug, 91
Whole-Food Oatmeal-
  Almond Mug Cake, 141
Winter, fruit availability
  in, 58, 70

X
Xylitol, 20–21

Y
Yellow cakes with liquors, 122
Yellow Mug Cake, 39

CPSIA information can be obtained
at www.ICGtesting.com
Printed in the USA
BVOW10s0459091117

499882BV00010B/63/P